AFRICAN FIREBRAND
Kenyatta of Kenya

An African shepherd boy, son of a tribal farmer, grandson of a rain-making magician, Jomo Kenyatta rose to become the sophisticated leader of his nation and one of the greatest forces for progress in a continent swept by the winds of change. As a boy, he saw his country taken over by white settlers, his people turned into second-class citizens. Although filled with reverence for his tribal heritage, he educated himself for the future, and abandoned a distinguished scholarly career in England to lead his people's struggle for freedom. Caught between the arrogance of the British and the violent extremism of the Mau-Mau rebels, he refused to side with either. After years of jail and persecution as a dangerous firebrand, he was given the near-impossible task of governing his nation. He has largely ended tribal and racial strife in Kenya, and has proved to be a shield, not a sword, for the whites who had feared him.

Books by Jules Archer

AFRICAN FIREBRAND
Kenyatta of Kenya
BATTLEFIELD PRESIDENT
Dwight D. Eisenhower
FIGHTING JOURNALIST
Horace Greeley
FRONT-LINE GENERAL
Douglas MacArthur
MAN OF STEEL
Joseph Stalin
RED REBEL
Tito of Yugoslavia
SCIENCE EXPLORER
Roy Chapman Andrews
TWENTIETH-CENTURY CAESAR
Benito Mussolini
WORLD CITIZEN
Woodrow Wilson
ANGRY ABOLITIONIST
William Lloyd Garrison

AFRICAN FIREBRAND
Kenyatta of Kenya

by Jules Archer

JULIAN MESSNER NEW YORK

Published simultaneously in the United States and Canada by
Julian Messner, a division of Simon & Schuster, Inc.,
1 West 39 Street, New York, N.Y. 10018. All rights reserved.

To
Evelyn and Rudy Wittels
in deep appreciation

Printed in the United States of America
SBN 671-32061-0 Cloth Trade
    671-32062-9 MCE
Library of Congress Catalog Card No. 69-12103

1562107

Contents

	Introduction	7
1	Boy with Spear	11
2	The White Man Comes	21
3	Struggles in Nairobi	31
4	Black Man in White Europe	43
5	Kenyatta Comes Home	55
6	Mau Mau!	67
7	"Mau Mau? What Is That?"	79
8	The Trial of Burning Spear	91
9	Desert Prisoner	103
10	*"Uhuru* Kenyatta! *Uhuru* Kenya!"	115
11	A Man Is Freed	127
12	A Nation Is Freed	139
13	*"Harambee!"*	151
14	Challenge to the Lion	163
15	Kenyatta's Country, Today and Tomorrow	175
	Suggested Further Reading	186
	Index	187

Introduction

THE STORY OF JOMO KENYATTA, WHO FOUGHT WHITE racism in his native Kenya, has special overtones for Americans today. He, like the late Dr. Martin Luther King in America, urged the white government of his country to end racial discrimination in schools, jobs and living conditions. Like King, too, Kenyatta warned the government that if it refused to heed the nonviolent protests he led, black people would lose hope and turn to leaders who urged violence as the only way to win redress of their grievances.

Kenyatta failed, as King had failed, to persuade the white leaders of his government. The result in both cases was chaos. In Kenya a savage African tribal movement called Mau Mau plunged the country into a racial bloodbath. In the United States, Black Nationalists pushed aside nonviolent Negro leaders. City after city began to suffer fire-bombings, looting and riots.

Kenya's white colonial government went bankrupt fighting a bitter racial war that ended in black African control of the country. The outcome of America's stormy racial conflict still lies in the future.

The parallel is not a perfect one, of course. Kenya was a small African colony; the United States is a great, independent major power. In white-controlled colonial Kenya, there was only one white man to every hundred black Africans. In the United States today there are ten white men for every Negro; white power far outweighs black power. But what happened in Kenya should serve as a grim warning to Americans that such a tragedy must not be allowed to happen here. White America must listen to black America.

Opponents of full equality for the Negro base their opposition on a belief in the black man's inferiority and uncivilized behavior. The white settlers who controlled the colonial government of Kenya shared this belief. They cited the outbreak of Mau Mau terrorism as proof that they had been justified in setting up a society that practiced racial discrimination.

A remarkable analysis came from Dr. Frantz Fanon, a distinguished Negro psychiatrist born in Martinique. In a book called *The Wretched of the Earth,* he set forth the view that African natives could be expected to behave in precisely the way that white settlers described them. Called animals, Fanon said, they would behave like animals. Called barbarians, they would behave barbarously. Fanon developed this insight from the observation by Jean-Paul Sartre that "we become what we are called."

Fanon went a step further and said that this development was not only inevitable but the "duty" of black people. In no other way, he wrote, could black people protect themselves from abuse and persecution. White people had to understand that the white's *own* attitudes would determine whether there would be Mau Mau in the country, or rioting, looting and burning in the cities. Whites who persisted in scorning black people as inferiors to be kept out of white neighborhoods, discriminated against in jobs, called "boy" and clubbed by police should not be surprised when those same people turned to dope, crime and arson in desperation.

If you keep telling a man he is no good, Fanon pointed out, it will not be long before you convince him. On the other hand, if whites treated black people as humanly and fairly as they treated themselves, the country could expect a new generation of law-abiding black people.

A remarkable leader like Jomo Kenyatta had a great deal to say to black people all over the world, including Negroes in the United States. He told them that they had the right to demand equal treatment with the white man, to be given educational opportunities, to share in the prosperity they helped to create by their labor.

But he also warned them against following demagogues who promised them something for nothing. "It is a sad mistake," he told his people, "to think that you can get more food, more hospitals or schools by crying 'Communism.'" The only way, Kenyatta taught, was hard work and self-help.

The hour is getting late for a fresh look at the priorities of America's commitments. As Martin Luther King pointed out before he was assassinated, Negro Americans were growing deeply impatient with a nation that claimed it was too poor to afford the money the Kerner Commission insisted had to be spent to correct the injustices Negroes had suffered in America for over three centuries.

America's young people will soon constitute a majority of the nation's voters. They are a better-educated generation, largely free of the racial stereotypes and prejudices of older generations. Perhaps they will be able to create a new multiracial society in which black, white, Mexican, Puerto Rican and American Indian can share America in friendship, cooperation, peace and plenty.

The author is indebted to the Permanent Mission of the Republic of Kenya to the UN for source material on the life and career of President Kenyatta. Acknowledgment is also made for background notes on Kenya released by the US Department of State. Special acknowledgment is due Sabena Belgian World Airlines, whose superbly comfortable flights to Africa constitute one of the important air bridges between the Western world and the fascinating Dark Continent, rapidly becoming an exotic tourist favorite.

A word on Kikuyu spelling, based on the authority of Jomo Kenyatta himself. The spelling used in this book is the commonly accepted European version. Native spelling, insofar as there is one in a language principally verbal, would term the tribe as *Gikuyu,* pronounced "Gekoyo."

Actually, *Gikuyu* refers to the country; *Mu-Gikuyu* is a member of the tribe; *A-Gikuyu* is the plural form. But to avoid driving confused readers into the hills, I have used the simple European version, *Kikuyu,* to encompass all these shades of meaning. What is important is not the way *Kikuyu* spell themselves, but the vital message they have for us.

JULES ARCHER

PINE PLAINS
NEW YORK

10

Boy with Spear

EACH DAY OF HIS YOUTH THE EYES OF JOMO KENYATTA turned in awe toward smoke-purple Mount Kenya, whose snowcapped peak rose 17,000 feet out of the steaming equator. On top of the mysterious volcanic mountain that his tribe called Kere-Nyaga lived Ngai, god of the Kikuyu people. Kenyatta's parents taught him to gaze at the holy place once every morning, when its ice field sparkled in the brilliant tropical sunshine, and once every evening, when a starry black sky and powerful moon revealed Ngai brooding palely over a sleeping Africa.

The child who would one day be worshipped by his people even as they worshipped Ngai was born in the thatched-hut village of Ichaweri in the White Highlands, a Kikuyu tribal area north of what is now Nairobi, capital of Kenya. His tribal name was Kamau wa Ngengi —Kamau son of Ngengi. Evidence suggests 1890 as his birthdate, although in 1952 he testified in court, "I do not know when I was born—what date, what month or what year—but I think I am over fifty."

He was the first son of a farmer with several wives. Ngengi, his father, lived in his own *thingira* (men's hut), where he entertained friends and visitors. His wives each had a separate *nymoba* (woman's hut), where they lived with their children. Kamau did not feel deprived because he had to share his father with other families. Kikuyu wives and children regarded each other as relatives and lived as a unit.

"To live with others," Kamau's mother told him, "is to share and to have mercy for one another. It is only witchdoctors who live and eat alone." In addition to looking after her hut, garden and children, she took her turn with other wives in caring for their husband, collecting his firewood and feeding his sheep and goats.

Kamau assured his brother Moigai that when they grew up, they too would prove themselves men like their father and develop a homestead with many dutiful wives.

Kamau's homeland of Kenya, about the size of Texas, rolled up from low plains adjacent to the Indian Ocean to grassy inland plateaus 5,500 feet above sea level. Kamau grew up in these highlands invigorated by bright sunshine and cool, clear air. There was plenty of water for the extremely fertile soil, and the land was beautiful. The highlands contrasted sharply with the bleak, arid scrubland to the north that constituted three fifths of Kenya.

Kamau's people, the Kikuyu, made up a fifth of Kenya's 9,000,000 Africans. They were the largest single tribe in the country—Bantus who had wandered into Kenya from West and Central Africa centuries earlier. A tall, broad-shouldered people, they tilled the soil and sometimes lived by hunting in the forests.

They were feared by other tribes, especially the Luo, who made up 14 percent of the population, and the Baluhya and Kamba (12 percent each). These tribes considered the Kikuyu a sullen, aggressive people, and distrusted them. But white people who knew the Kikuyu well found them an advanced, intelligent tribe of such sensitivity that no parent ever raised his hand to a child.

Spoiled by doting sisters, cousins and his father's wives, Kamau thoroughly enjoyed his childhood. The round hut he lived in with his mother in Ichaweri had wooden walls and a grass-thatched roof. About thirty-six feet in diameter, it had a fireplace in the center. Center poles supported the roof, bracing partitions that divided the hut into rooms. The largest room sheltered sheep and goats at night. Next to it, clockwise, came his mother's room, the storeroom, his sisters' room, the room he shared with his brother Moigai, and the *gecego* for fattening livestock.

From his earliest years Kamau imbibed the spirit of industry and energy that characterized Kikuyu life. He watched his father and other men cut timber to build huts and fences, clear the bush to cultivate new fields, plow the soil with digging sticks, cut drainage ditches, herd livestock, slaughter livestock for food, prepare skins for clothing, cut and peel sugarcane, stand guard at night to protect bananas and yams from wild animal raids.

He watched his mother and other women as they cut grass for thatching, plastered hut walls with clay or manure, cooked, fetched river water and firewood, planted maize, beans, millet and sweet potato vines, harvested crops, made dresses, wove baskets, made pottery, ground corn and millet in wooden mortars, made gruel, pounded sugarcane to make Kikuyu beer. Even great-grandmothers made themselves useful, sitting on little platforms to scare birds away from the gardens.

From as early as he could remember, Kamau was trained for his tribal role in agriculture and herding. "You must only do men's things," his mother cautioned him. "No woman would marry you if you can do women's work, because then what use would she be in the marriage?"

As soon as he was old enough to handle a digging

stick, he was given a small garden of his own to practice planting yams and sugarcane. When he was able to distinguish weeds from crops, he was sometimes allowed to join the weeding teams of ten or more friends who would cultivate each other's fields in the morning, then spend the afternoon feasting and singing. Kamau loved the sound of their laughter, which grew more uproarious as the sugarcane beer ebbed away.

He loved even more the festivities of seasonal day songs and dances, when ceremonial drums beat out hypnotic rhythms for a *kebata* celebration. His eyes glowed as he watched Kikuyu warriors, large rattles tied below their knees, display their agility with spears and shields, leaping about in astonishing high jumps and springing strides. One day he, too, would take part in the *kebata* dances, jumping higher and farther than anyone else!

There were two harvests a year. While Kamau's mother was busy harvesting and carrying the grain home, his father would clean the fields, burn stalks and spread the ashes as fertilizer. Between harvests Kamau would accompany his mother to village markets to exchange surplus grains for animal skins, bracelets, earrings, knives or whatever else the family needed.

Sometimes he went to the marketplace with his father when Ngengi wanted to trade sheep for goats, or goats for a cow. With awe he would watch a medicine man administer the required oath to both traders. Sipping a magic concoction, they would swear, "If the property I am now claiming is not mine, let this symbol of truth kill me." Oathing played much the same role in Kikuyu life that swearing on the Bible in court plays in Western society. Few Kikuyu dared violate an oath once they had sworn it.

By Ichaweri standards, Kamau's father was not badly off. Ngengi owned enough sheep, goats and cattle to have been able to afford the bride price for many wives. A cow was valued at ten sheep or goats, an ox at five. The price of everything in Kikuyuland, including wives, was determined in animal units.

Kamau regarded his father with mingled pride and awe. Like all heads of family among the Kikuyu, Ngengi exercised great power over his wives and children. His consent had to be obtained before Kamau could join a feast, undergo manhood rites or obtain a wife. Supreme ruler of the family, he was respected and obeyed by all who called him father or husband.

As the oldest son, Kamau was his father's favorite. A good-natured and likable child, he was not above getting into mischief. He would steal sugarcane and maize, and spy on the dances of his elders. Once he peeped at the women making pottery at the molding place taboo to men, whose presence was said to spoil the pots by causing them to break while being baked on the fire.

The cracking of two pots as he watched from behind a bush caused some of the women to glare about suspiciously. Kamau beat a silent but hasty retreat.

Most of the games he played were imitations of the adult life of the tribe. Playing the marriage game, he would build play huts with the boys while their "wives" plaited baskets of grass, made little clay pots and prepared imaginary meals.

But most of all he enjoyed mimicking Kikuyu warriors in tribal clashes with the Masai and Somali. Using a wooden spear and a shield made of banana tree bark, he took part in mock battles with boys of other districts. In athletic contests he won respect for his strength and prowess in wrestling, running, jumping, lifting weights and throwing clubs.

His sisters spent their play time learning how to win and please a future husband—how to lower their eyes and voice when talking to males in public; how to treat strangers with polite suspicion; how to cook, grind and perform other chores that would make them choice catches.

Kamau's mother was his earliest and most constant teacher. Every evening after supper, as darkness fell over the grassy plains, she would light the fire in their hut and gather her children around it to teach them tribal laws, customs and legends. Her husky voice, singing about them in Kikuyu folk songs, haunted Kamau's memory all his life and later helped to make him world-famous.

Little Kamau enjoyed the riddles and puzzles posed by his mother to test her children's learning about Kikuyu history and customs. Almost always he was the first to shout out the answers. When his proud mother entered him in tribal competitions with other children of his age group, Kamau's performances in song and dance of the folklore she had taught him were voted best.

Kamau's practical education was supplied by his father. Following Ngengi through garden, field and forest, he learned many useful things—how to handle his digging stick; which plants were antidotes for snakebite; which wild fruits were poisonous and which edible; where the family and clan boundaries were; how to recognize family livestock by color and horns.

Once his father arranged to mix two or three herds from different homesteads, testing Kamau by making him pick out all the family's animals. Kamau correctly identified all but one goat that he could not find. Ngengi made him go through the herd over and over until he finally located the elusive goat behind a bush, where it had been tethered to test his powers of observation. When the family flock was entrusted to him, Kamau trained his younger brothers the same way.

His eighth year was a proud one. To protect the herd from prowling lions and leopards, he was given his first bow and arrow. Wearing a new tanned goatskin and carrying his weapon conspicuously, Kamau shot many an arrow at rustling grass and bushes in the hope they concealed a predator.

When he was ten he advanced from childhood to boyhood by having his earlobes pierced. As the firstborn son of a first wife, he was now taken into his father's confidence and taught the rules governing the land Ngengi owned. By tribal custom he was now allowed to serve his father as a witness in land transactions and disputes. After his father's death, he would become a *moramati* (trustee), acting as guardian of the land for the whole family group.

British misunderstanding of this custom of *moramati* was to have terrible consequences for all of Kenya. The Kikuyu system of land tenure was not tribal ownership. No chief or group of chiefs was allowed to sell any land except that which was personally owned. Nor could any *moramati* sell family land without the agreement of all his brothers. In effect, this system made it almost impossible for the white man legally to buy any large tract of Kikuyu land.

While they held and worked the land, Kamau's people were a prosperous, closely knit, deeply religious and smoothly run society. Kamau often recited with fervor the Kikuyu adage: "I and my grandfather are one: I and my brother are one: I and my wife are one."

A second unifying principle that bound Kamau to his people was the age-group system. Every Kikuyu youth belonged to a fraternity of other youths his own age. Age groups between eighteen and forty served as the *aneke* (warrior class), controlled and supervised by a council of ruling elders. The council laid down strict criminal and civil laws for the tribe. There was very little crime or immorality among the law-abiding Kikuyu.

Kamau grew up indoctrinated with the tribe's strong community spirit. He joined his father and uncles in gardening for aged neighbors, building houses for sick or crippled tribesmen. With his age group, he helped fight for or pay the fine of any member of their group in trouble. He always knew that if he ever needed them, his fellow tribesmen would be just as quick to come to his aid. Any Kikuyu who lived and worked for himself alone was ostracized.

Kamau loved above all else to visit with his paternal grandfather, Kongo wa Magana, who had once led southern Kikuyu warriors against Masai on the borders of Kenya and what is now Tanzania. In the eyes of white missionaries, his grandfather was a witch doctor or medicine man, but this was inaccurate. Kongo was a magician and tribal wise man who foretold the future, advised on war strategy, provided war charms and served as military priest.

As tribal wars grew fewer, he was called upon more and more to make rain, remove evil spells, bless a hunting expedition, predict the future and communicate with dead tribal ancestors as well as the gods. His contacts with the spirit world were relied upon to make certain it was safe to leave a village to work, or to find out where an ox had strayed or who had made off with a stolen hoe.

Kamau was in great awe of his grandfather's magical powers, and swore later that he had witnessed the performance of successful rites of magic many times. "In traveling about with him and carrying his bag of equipment," he wrote years later, "I served a kind of apprenticeship in the principles of the art." Trotting up and down the steep ridges of Kikuyuland at his grandfather's heels, through pasturelands, salt licks, woodlands and forests, Kamau saw much that he marveled at. He never doubted that Kongo was, indeed, in contact with the spirits of dead tribesmen floating in the skies over Kenya.

"In the case of the ceremony in which I took part," Kamau recalled years later, "I well remember that our prayers were quickly answered, for even before the sacred fires had ceased to burn, torrential rain came upon us. We were soaked, and it will not be easy for me to forget the walk home in the downpour."

Even when he became one of the most sophisticated statesmen of Africa, he never lost the strong streak of tribal mysticism he developed watching the wonders performed by his grandfather, the magician Kongo wa Magana.

2 ⟨⟨⟨⟨⟨⟨⟨⟨⟨⟨⟨⟨⟨⟨⟨⟨⟨⟨⟨

The White Man Comes

ONE DAY KAMAU'S GRANDFATHER TOOK HIM TO VISIT A clan of Kikuyu smiths. He watched them wash iron ore from river sands, dry it and smelt it over charcoal fires. Then they hammered blooms of glowing iron into spears, digging and clearing knives, arrowheads and axes. To Kamau's delight a spear he was watching made was suddenly handed to him when it was finished.

"It is yours, grandson of Kongo," the smith smiled. "Your grandfather ordered it for a brave young lion."

Kamau treasured the spear and kept it by him lovingly as he herded cattle and tilled his grandfather's *shamba* (farm) on a steep, red-earthed ridge in Kikuyuland. He hefted it proudly on jungle trips with Kongo, absorbing the old seer's wisdom about wild animal habits, edible birds, trees good for building or ideal as beehives. Kamau enjoyed his stays with his grandfather so much that he would put off for days the time when his mother expected him to return to Ichaweri.

Of all the stories told him by Kongo, the one that impressed him most dealt with a great magician named Mogo, whose duty it was to predict the future and advise the Kikuyu nation how to prepare for it. One morning Mogo woke up trembling and speechless from a vision in his sleep. He told the council of elders that Ngai had taken him to the peak of Kere-Nyaga to hear prophecies. Ngai warned that a famine would overtake Kikuyuland, after which strangers would come, their bodies the color of frog bellies and dressed like butterflies. They would carry magic killing sticks that would produce fire. They would bring in an iron snake with as many legs as a centipede, and it would stretch across the nation spitting fire. This would mark the beginning of great suffering for all the tribes of Kenya—the Kikuyu most of all.

Mogo warned the elders that the Kikuyu must not try to fight the strangers. They would only be killed by the magic sticks. And neither spears nor arrows would penetrate the hide of the iron snake. The strangers should be treated with polite suspicion and not allowed to get too close to Kikuyu homesteads, or they would seize the tribe's lands.

Mogo's predictions had begun to come true, Kongo told his enthralled grandson, about the time Kamau had been born. Bad times caused by cattle disease, drought and a locust invasion had caused a famine that drove many Kikuyu, Masai and Kamba from their homesteads in search of food.

Then the white Europeans had begun to arrive in Kenya. Now they were building the great iron centipede across southern Kenya from Mombasa on the coast to Victoria Nyanza (Lake Victoria) in the west. The great question now, Kongo said somberly, was whether the last of Mogo's predictions would also come to pass— seizure of the Kikuyu lands. If it did, terrible days lay ahead.

It was only years later that Kamau completely understood what had happened to his homeland when he was a child. The first whites had come to Kenya in the early 1890's following a report by an English explorer who described enthusiastically a virgin country that "as far as the eye could see was one vast garden." Until then Kenya had only been visited by Arabs, who had colonized along the coast in the eighth century, and by Portuguese traders in the fifteenth century.

Most of coastal East Africa was, by the 1880's, under the nominal rule of the Sultan of Zanzibar. In 1887 he granted the British East Africa Company a fifty-year trading concession. But the first traders found that the long supply line inland was too vulnerable to native attack. At their urging the British government took over, establishing a protectorate in Kenya and Uganda.

The next step was to open up Kenya with a railroad. The British imported 35,000 laborers from India. Despite tropical diseases, man-eating lions, elephant stampedes and unpredictable rhinos, the Indians pushed tracks west from Mombasa. Their greatest hazard was the angry tribes of Kenya, who attacked them with poisoned darts and arrows.

The Nandi raided track-building caravans for steel rails, bolts, spikes and other prizes. British-led native forces, sent out to attack the Nandi, murdered the tribe's chief. The Nandi were then swept off their land onto a reserve distant from the railway. Several other tribes had to be fought and subdued the same way.

When the track-laying caravans reached Kikuyuland, Chief Waiyaki and other Kikuyu leaders entered into a treaty of friendship with the strangers, supplying them with food and giving them the right to build forts for trading. But the railway workers displayed a fatal disdain for the "savages," robbing their crops, violating their laws and shooting those who protested. Railroad officials looked the other way.

Kikuyu warriors finally attacked the caravans, twice overrunning and burning Fort Dagoretti. The British commissioner decided that Kamau's people had to be taught a lesson. The Kikuyu were fined fifty goats daily as food for the Indian laborers, and three hundred tribesmen were compelled to rebuild Fort Dagoretti. Chief Waiyaki was seized and deported from the highlands. When he died mysteriously on the way to Mombasa, the outraged Kikuyu refused to supply the Europeans with any more food, firewood or water.

They hoped by this boycott to force the intruders out of their lands. Instead the British simply sent out military parties to confiscate whatever they needed.

Ironically, when the railroad was finally pushed through to completion in 1903, there simply weren't enough European settlers in Kenya to make its use profitable. Although most of the Indian laborers decided to remain in Kenya, a committee of twenty-two pioneer Englishmen decided that what the colony needed was British immigration to develop its agricultural and mining resources.

In January, 1902, they met in the raw new town of Nairobi to press three demands on the resident commissioner—offer free land grants to new British settlers for model farms; end Indian immigration; put Kenya's tribes under control—and the demands were granted.

Thousands of amateur farmers came from cramped England, lured by free fertile land on a new frontier with a railroad to ship their crops and cattle to the coast for export. With them came missionaries, black-sheep sons of nobility, adventure-seekers and experienced South African farmers.

The climate was so cool and pleasant, and the rolling downs looked so much like England's own beautiful countryside, that the British immigrants determined to make Kenya their permanent home. They began to establish homesteads on fertile highlands they found empty, unaware or not caring that these lands belonged to Kikuyu who had been forced to leave them temporarily because of famine to seek food in the forests.

The English settlers assumed that those Kikuyu who had not left their highlands were without any concept of land ownership, like the Bantu. Some settlers paid the Kikuyu a handful of shillings for unoccupied acres of farmland near native villages, considering that they had thus bought permanent legal title to these valuable thousands of acres.

But those Kikuyu thought they were merely renting the lands, as they sometimes did among themselves. The lands belonged either to absent tribesmen, and were being held in trust for the family by a *moramati*, or to a chief whose whole clan used them for district meetings and celebrations, pastures, grazing lands, salt licks and woodlands.

Even such a chief could not legally sell his lands except after long and elaborate ceremonies involving the adoption of the buyer into the clan. This was necessary because the Kikuyu revered the land as sacred. Their ancestors were buried in it, and only after a buyer became a blood brother, and swore great oaths to continue ceremonials honoring the ancestral spirits, could the land be legally transferred.

The British knew or cared nothing about Kikuyu tribal law. They simply saw "unoccupied" land and occupied it. Those uneducated Kikuyu who accepted a pittance for adjacent land simply thought the white men needed it temporarily for trading purposes, and would soon move on.

They were, in any event, in no position to resist the strangers with frog-belly skins who dressed like butterflies and carried deadly magic killing sticks. The British herded them off the highlands into reserves, using them as a pool of cheap labor to work the farms that once had belonged to them and to absent members of the tribe.

This tragic development contained the seeds of the savage Mau Mau bloodbath that was to bring about the ordeal of Kamau wa Ngengi, the boy later known as Jomo Kenyatta.

Not all white settlers were blind to the danger. As early as 1902 Captain Meinertzhagen of the King's African Rifles in Kenya warned Commissioner Sir Charles Eliot, "Kikuyu are the most intelligent of the African tribes I have met. Therefore they will be the most . . . susceptible to subversive activities. They will be the first to demand freedom . . . and in the end, cause a lot of trouble."

But Eliot only shrugged off Meinertzhagen's foreboding. "We are not destroying any old or interesting system," he denied, "but simply introducing order into blank, brutal barbarism. In any event, the interests of Africans cannot be admitted to be paramount over the interests of Europeans."

Even this blunt spokesman for British imperialism was not emphatic enough for the white settlers of Kenya, who demanded an iron-fisted colonial policy. Their spokesman and social leader was Lieutenant Colonel Ewart Scott Grogan, DSO, who began farming half a million acres of sisal and fruit in what became known as the White Highlands of Kikuyuland in 1904.

"The partition of occupation of Africa with a view to sound colonization," he had said in 1900, "is the obvious duty of the nations that form the vanguard of civilization."

Four years later he insisted that the native African wasn't being exploited just because he was handled with "a little firmness" to transform him from "a useless and dangerous brute into a source of benefit to the country and satisfaction to himself." Both "Grogs" Grogan and Commissioner Eliot, relaxing together at the restricted bar in Nairobi, would have been vastly amused by any suggestion that Kikuyu society was based on a sophisticated, religious and humane culture that they did not even suspect existed.

Kamau's uneasiness about the changes taking place in Kikuyuland first developed while he was herding cattle on the pasture around a sacred tree near Ichaweri. It dawned on him with a shock that this was now the only sacred tree left in the neighborhood. All the others he knew about had been cut down to clear the land for cultivation by the new British settlers in the region.

Only around this tree was it still possible for his people to make rain sacrifices or appeal for help to Ngai on the heights of Mount Kenya. Even this tree, Kamau knew, might soon be toppled. He had heard some Kikuyu, missionary converts, talk of cutting down this last "influence of Satan" to make room for the power of their new white god.

Herding his flocks, Kamau watched in growing sadness as his people came to the sacred tree to lament, *"Kikuyu harea kaeri kiano-imaho."* ("The Kikuyu are no longer where they used to be.") Why, he wondered, did Ngai allow the white strangers with the killing sticks to drive his people from their lands? Was the whites' god stronger than Ngai?

Musing over the paradox, he would accompany his thoughts with reflective notes on a flute made of the bark of a shrub branch. His improvised melodies pleased women working in nearby fields, who often sent appreciative presents of food and drink to his mother's hut for his having brightened their hours of work.

When Kamau was ten he was attacked by jiggers,

insects that bore into his feet while he moved through tall grass. His efforts to remove them were unsuccessful, and he came down with a severe spinal disease. The village witch doctor was summoned. His medicine proved unsuccessful, even though Ngengi sacrificed a choice sheep and gave a beer-drinking party to placate offended ancestral spirits who were believed to be responsible.

Both Ngengi and Kamau were startled when Kamau's mother insisted that he be taken to a Church of Scotland mission, to give the white man's magic a chance to cure him. Ngengi gave grudging consent, and Kamau was carried to Fort Hall near Nairobi. Medically trained missionaries quickly and correctly diagnosed his condition, and fortunately had the drugs to treat it. Kamau made a swift recovery.

Shaken and impressed by the white man's magic that had succeeded where the efforts of a witch doctor had failed, Kamau agreed to the missionaries' offer to teach him the white man's magic of reading and writing strange symbols that could communicate ideas without a word being spoken.

The mission proved a turning point in Kamau's life. To signalize his crossover into the white culture, he was baptized under the name of Johnstone Kamau. He not only learned to read and write English, but also was trained in carpentry and taught to be a kitchen hand.

The missionary who taught him seemed to the African youth a young white god. Kamau was deeply impressed with his smart clothes and shoes, his watch and amazing bicycle. Was it possible that Kamau, too, might one day own such magnificent things? He put all of his energy into learning, and rapidly became the school's star pupil. With painstaking care he copied his teacher's clean fingernails and manner of speaking, walking and gesturing.

He reflected deeply over the Church of Scotland's instructions for behavior toward parents, elders and a supreme being. These ideas were vastly different from those his own people had taught him. He grew skeptical about accepting white culture uncritically, because he realized how little the white man understood about Kenya's black culture.

He was suspended between two worlds—not prepared to accept white Christianity uncritically, yet no longer able to believe fully in tribal taboos and superstitions. Part of the trouble, he realized, was the communication barrier. The whites who scorned to learn Kikuyu could not understand his people's culture. To master European ideas, Africans had only the jargon of Swahili, a Bantu-based language laced with Arabic, English and native dialects.

Not everyone spoke Swahili, but in almost every village of Kenya there was someone who understood it. To close the communication gap, Kamau not only mastered Swahili but also became a polished English linguist. He learned how to interpret black ideas to whites, and white ideas to blacks.

"It is important for the European teacher to realize," he wrote, "that he is not pouring new wine into new bottles, but into very old bottles. . . . The assumption of knowing the African's mind has been very often heard in the usual phraseology: 'I have lived for many years amongst the Africans and I know them well.' Yet this is far from the actual fact, for there is a great difference between 'living' among a people and 'knowing' them."

It was the fatal flaw in the white missionary that he knew little of Kikuyu culture, and did not pause to question whether the white man's values were suitable for Africans.

"The natives were not as savage and degraded as supposed," wrote Daniel Thwaite in *Seething African Pot*, "and anyway, the more difficult they were to deal with, the better their teachers should have been." The blunt truth was that the missionaries had been sent to break up an African social structure whose complexity they did not appreciate.

Their greatest failure was Johnstone Kamau.

3 ‹‹‹‹‹‹‹‹‹‹‹‹‹‹‹‹‹‹‹‹‹

Struggles in Nairobi

THE YOUNG AFRICAN WAS RELUCTANT TO PART WITH THE sacred tribal taboos he had been taught—never to pray to Ngai until he had first been cleansed of sin by a medicine man; never to raise his eyes to Mount Kenya when Ngai sent out white flashes of anger; always to listen in awe to Ngai's rumbled reproach.

But he found himself floundering between two worlds—one white, one black. He was bemused to find that the Lord God of the Old Testament seemed to have a lot in common with Ngai. Yet there were many contradictions in the Christian teaching. Did not the most respected elders of the Bible practice polygamy? Yet the missionaries said that it was immoral for a man to have more than one wife.

When he questioned this paradox, the missionary teacher told him sharply that it was wrong for him to do so because he could not possibly understand the explanation. Perhaps, Kamau persisted, but why did the Church of Scotland insist that every African with more than one family abandon all his wives and children except the first family? Was this not a terrible injustice and unkindness to many wives and innocent children? Was this Christian love?

The missionaries quickly cooled toward the prickly, probing mind of Johnstone Kamau, whose embarrassing questions they learned to dread. They finally ordered him to be silent. He did not, however, turn hostile toward them.

"Missionaries have done a lot of good work," he told BBC interviewer John Freeman in 1963, "because it was through the missionary that many of the Kikuyu got their first education . . . and were able to learn how to read and write. Because the missionary wanted them to be able to read the Bible. . . . Also, the medical side of it: the missionary did very well."

But, he added, "at the same time I think the missionaries . . . did not understand the value of the African custom, and many of them tried to stamp out some of the customs without knowing the part they play in the life of the Kikuyu. . . . They upset the life of the people."

By turning young Kikuyu against their traditions—polygamy, coming-of-age rites, tribal oaths, pagan gods and ceremonials—the missionaries inadvertently weakened the control of Kikuyu elders and the age-group system over the behavior of the young.

More and more Kikuyu deserted the villages—some for missionary school, but most to seek the white man's way of life in the growing cities. Kikuyu family life began to deteriorate. In its place were the chaos and disillusionment of young blacks jobless in city slums, and of adult Kikuyu adrift as squatters or on reserves.

To make matters worse, the more polygamous marriages the missionaries prevented or broke up as "immoral," the more Kikuyu women were forced to do without husbands. Compelled to leave the villages and reserves to search for city jobs, they frequently could not find work and were forced to resort to prostitution to keep themselves alive.

An early clash developed between the Colonists' Association, the local power structure of the white settlers, and the British Colonial Office. The settlers invoked harsh measures against the Kikuyu to teach them quickly who was master in Kenya. The commissioner disapproved, feeling that only benevolence justified British imperialism.

In 1906 the Colonists' Association passed a Masters' and Servants' Ordinance punishing any natives who refused to work on white settlers' farms. A year later Colonel Grogan, the Association's president, took part in publicly flogging three recalcitrant Kikuyu in front of the Nairobi Courthouse.

The angered Colonial Office promptly issued a decree nullifying the slave ordinance and assuring natives that they need not work for the settlers unless they wanted to. Ignoring the commissioner, the settlers continued to treat the Kikuyu as they pleased. Some were humane, but many kicked or whipped Africans who displeased them by being slow when called or by forgetting to doff their hats in respect.

The white settlers were equally contemptuous of the East Indians, and would not let them buy land in the White Highlands. "The Indian standard of living is much too low," Grogan asserted, "and this would hardly be a help in civilizing the blacks to make them understand why persons of color must remain within their own society."

A new Legislative Council controlled by the settlers passed laws dividing Kenya into three sharply separate groups of a caste system—white, Indian and black. Only whites were permitted in the hotels, restaurants and churches of Nairobi and Mombasa. None but whites were permitted to serve as representatives on the Council.

The exclusion of Indians from the Council infuriated

the new Undersecretary of State for the Colonies in London. Coming to Kenya, Winston Churchill told the Council, "There can be no reason for excluding this large and meritorious class. Begin early to instil good principles in the East Africa Protectorate!" He also warned the Council to heed Kikuyu grievances about the land.

"After all," he growled, "it's *their* Africa."

Nevertheless, a true imperialist, Churchill supported Grogan and the settlers in their insistence upon forced labor. The Council promptly imposed heavy taxes upon the Kikuyu to compel them to leave their tribal villages and work for the settlers at starvation wages. To deprive them of an alternative, they were not allowed to grow coffee or other cash crops.

As a sop, natives who agreed to serve as cheap farm labor were allowed to cultivate small tracts for family use. The alternatives were starvation, joining the wretched ranks of jobless in the cities, or finding a low-paid job with a heavy proportion of the wages lost to taxes.

Kamau grew increasingly incensed at the injustices perpetrated against his people by the white settlers. In 1913 the Kikuyu were taxed almost half a million dollars, yet not a single nonmissionary school had been built for them. As for the missionary schools, Kamau was now convinced that their real purpose was not uplifting Africans, but controlling and training skilled labor for the white settlers.

For a while he worked at the Fort Hall mission as a kitchen boy and odd-job carpenter. But more and more he grew to feel that his heart and hands belonged to his people, not to the white strangers who had invaded their land.

In 1908 he returned to Ichaweri to solidify his ties with the tribe and take part in the age-group ceremony that would make him an adult tribesman of the Kikuyu. He would then be a blood brother of all Kikuyu born the same year, with a special kinship not unlike "the old school tie" that bound each class of English university alumni.

The thrill of African pride returned to him when he donned warrior costume and painted his body with red ochre. Like most of the other males in his age group, he exchanged flirtatious looks with girls undergoing the rites, dazzling in their beads, armlets and other adornments.

Kamau became leader of his age group by winning the race to a sacred tree and being the first to throw a wooden spear over it. When he was admitted into the council of junior warriors, his father presented him with the gifts of manhood—a new iron spear, a buffalo-hide shield, and a *simi,* or *panga,* the two-foot-long bush knife that first had been sanctified with the blood of a ceremonial sheep.

The age-group brotherhood faced Mount Kenya and raised their spears to Ngai. Kamau intoned with them, "We brandish our spears, symbol of our courageous and fighting spirit, never to retreat or abandon our hope, or run away from our comrades." And then he was a full-fledged tribesman.

But he continued to call himself Johnstone Kamau.

Working once more on his father's homestead, he found time to attend Kikuyu youth dances, where his huge muscular frame cut a proud figure. One pretty young girl set her cap for him, and Kamau found himself falling in love.

Ngengi pleaded his son's suit with her parents, taking along gifts of sugarcane beer. When they "reluctantly" gave their consent, the betrothal was sealed with a gift of thirty-four sheep by Ngengi to the bride's family. Soon

Kamau's female relatives went through the play-acting of kidnapping his bride from her garden, as watching villagers giggled in delight. She was brought to the wedding feast celebration where, for eight days, she dutifully sang her *kerero* (weeping) songs. Kamau, meanwhile, demonstrated his strength to her parents by such feats as carrying heavy loads of banana stalks and huge pots of water on his back. It was a fine wedding feast.

When they were man and wife by Kikuyu law, Kamau found himself curiously uneasy. The impact of his missionary training had been stronger than he thought. At his insistence his bride agreed to a second wedding ceremony in the Presbyterian Church at Nyeri, giving his marriage sanctity in the eyes of both his own people and the white Christians.

He wavered between staying on the land in Ichaweri and casting his fortunes among the whites of Nairobi, whose language he could speak and for whose service he had been trained. At first he remained on his father's farm, working some acreage his father gave him as his own. But then, in 1915, a new development outraged and upset him.

The Legislative Council forced the Colonial Office to agree to a Crown Land Ordinance. In effect this law expropriated "all land occupied by the African tribes of the Colony," making legal ownership possible only for white Britons. Africans like his father now occupied their lands only as "tenants-at-will" of the Crown, and could be kicked off onto native reserves whenever the government chose. The land most obviously threatened by the ordinance was the prized 16,000 square miles of Kikuyu acreage soon to become known, significantly, as the White Highlands.

Kamau watched bitterly as some neighbors around him were dispossessed of their farms and moved onto reserves that were thinly disguised concentration camps. By 1919 the intolerably crowded reserves were divided into garden plots so tiny and eroded as to be incapable of supporting the families compelled to depend upon them.

Some Kikuyu died of starvation. Almost as badly off were the 110,000 members of the tribe living as poor squatters on the white plantations, tolerated only as long as they continued to be willing to serve as cheap farm labor.

Thousands who rejected a wretched life on the reserves or plantations sought survival among the squalid slum shacks of the cities. But here whites held all the key posts, and Indians all the clerical and skilled labor jobs. When an African could find city employment, it was usually only as a servant or manual laborer at low wages. Even this pay fell to starvation level during the depression of 1920.

All laws were passed and enforced with one chief objective—to consolidate the power of a white minority by tightening their control over a black population of 7,000,000. The Colonists' Association firmly believed that unless they kept the lid firmly clamped on African aspirations, a black explosion would blow every white man out of Kenya.

Kamau knew that the only hope for his people lay in education. Literacy would give them the knowledge to understand what was being done to them, why and what they had to do to protect their society. The missionaries who had taught him to read and write had expanded his own horizons. Aware of this risk, the Colonists' Association was insisting that the missionaries restrict their education of natives to the minimum necessary for the use of Africans in the colonial machinery.

"The white man must be paramount," Grogan and his settlers resolved at a Convention of Associations held in 1919. "We must make the native a useful and contented citizen . . . give him reasonable education, especially technical, industrial and agricultural. The workshops on the farm should be the schools for education. Native labor is required for the country. . . . We must educate the native to come out of the reserve and work." The message was clear: the future of young Kikuyu was to be as toilers for the settlers.

Because of his mastery of English and Swahili, Kamau was chosen by Kikuyu Chief Kioi to act as interpreter in protesting the Crown Land Ordinance before the Nairobi Supreme Court. He sought to make the court understand that the "communal or tribal" land the government was confiscating was actually privately owned by *moramati* as trustees for their families.

"The government does not appreciate that in the Kikuyu religion our soil is considered sacred," Kamau told the court. "You must understand that is the kinship bond that unites our families, the foundation rock on which our whole tribal economy is built. The government is taking away not only our livelihood, but our whole Kikuyu way of life!"

He was incensed at the moral justification the white settlers used for confiscating the land—that the Kikuyu did not farm it properly and that it was necessary to confine them to reserves to stop tribal warfare. The government had just shown how civilized *it* was in fighting a great tribal war in Europe far more barbaric than any in Kenya.

Tens of thousands of Africans had been forced to fight and die in the King's forces during World War I. Those who returned to Kenya had been rewarded by finding their family's lands in the hands of the white settlers.

"The settlers speak as if it was somehow beneficial to an African to work for them instead of for himself," Kamau protested angrily, "and to make sure that he will receive this benefit they do their best to take away his land and leave him with no alternative. Along with his land they rob him of his government, condemn his religious ideas, and ignore his fundamental conceptions of justice and morals—all in the name of civilization and progress!"

Unmoved by Kamau's eloquent presentation of Chief Kioi's case against the Crown Land Ordinance, in 1921 the Nairobi Supreme Court upheld its legality. Now the way was clear to remove *all* African farmers from the White Highlands and satisfy the demand of Grogan and the settlers for more land.

Kamau, now thirty-one, knew that it was futile to try to remain in Ichaweri any longer. He left reluctantly for the bustling little shantytown of Nairobi, where East Indian shops offered bread, sugar, tea and liniment along a street so pitted that the rich settlers with cars had to weight them with heavy rocks to keep from bouncing around violently. There were frequent antelope prints in the dust where herds stampeded through the streets during the night.

Applying for a job at the Nairobi Municipality, Kamau was taken on as a clerk for the Public Works Department. Brainy, ambitious, gifted with an irresistible personal magnetism, he was soon promoted to the job of meter reader, then inspector, for the Nairobi waterworks.

But despite this success in the white man's world, he was determined not to "sell out" his people by abandoning their struggle against colonial injustice. To remind himself and others that he was first and foremost a Kikuyu, he took to wearing a colorful beaded belt known tribally as a *kenyatta*. Soon he was being called Johnstone Kenyatta, a name which pleased him for its African flavor.

Living now in the slum ghetto of Nairobi set aside for Africans, he became increasingly restless, missing his family in Ichaweri. He began attending local dances, where his articulate charm made him popular with Nairobi's native belles. For some time now his wife in Ichaweri, preoccupied with their small baby and the endless chores of Kikuyu domesticity, had encouraged him to look for a second wife. Now that his economic position had improved, he wooed and won a Nairobi girl and established a second family.

Living in town fueled Kenyatta's resentment toward the white elite. Sometimes when they were drunk they would race down the main street in rickshaws drawn by Africans, shooting out street lights or at the feet of frightened natives. Tough, touchy men, they often killed each other in gun duels at the white bars.

On their plantations in the Highlands, their chief sport was fox hunting. Brilliantly clad in tailed red jackets, they would mount their fine horses by stepping into the clasped hands of African servants. Elderly natives were addressed disdainfully as "boy" or even "monkey."

Kenyatta was one of the few exceptions to the code that reserved skilled and semiskilled jobs for the Asians. But he nevertheless tasted the full humiliation of Kenya's color bar. He could not enter any white hotel, restaurant, club or church. Despite his education, most Europeans disdained to speak to him in any language but Swahili, their own command of which was usually wretched.

The bitter thought persisted: *Millions of us, only ten thousand of them—yet they are our masters!*

He was not alone in his resentment. By this time a whole new young generation of Kikuyu had come of age since the first whites had arrived in Kenya. The contrast between white prosperity and black poverty made them deeply hostile. The Europeans had uprooted their civilization and destroyed tribal control. They had no way to support themselves on the land, no way to prove their manliness in hunts and tribal warfare. Stealing became commonplace as a means of both survival and demonstrating daring.

Kikuyu working on the white plantations stole milk and maize to keep their families from starving. They felt justified by the Kikuyu proverb, "He who is working in the cornfield should be fed there."

Frustration drove Kikuyu village chiefs and elders to join a new Kikuyu Association, organized by Harry Thuku, who worked as a telephone operator for the government. They agreed to follow his leadership in a political struggle to recover the stolen White Highlands. Thuku was financed by the sympathetic Indian editor of the *East African Chronicle,* who let him use the paper's car and office.

The Legislative Council grew alarmed as Thuku began traveling around Kenya addressing not only Kikuyu but also other tribes. He urged all natives to band together to end their "state of slavery" under the Europeans.

In March, 1922, Thuku was arrested and jailed in Nairobi. An angry crowd of Kikuyu demonstrated in protest outside the jail. Police fired into the crowd, killing twenty-five Africans. As a shock wave of excitement swept through the city, Thuku was rushed out of the prison to a reserve in the Northern Frontier District, where he was held in restriction.

A group of bitter young Kikuyu promptly organized a new militant organization called the Young Kikuyu Association (YKA). They appealed to Kenyatta to join them in leading a broad revolutionary struggle. Their aims were to recover the lost Kikuyu lands, free Harry Thuku, win African representation on the Legislative Council, compel real educational opportunities for Africans, end the hut tax on natives and stop exploitation of black labor by Europeans.

Although he knew that he would instantly become a marked man, Kenyatta did not hesitate. His people needed a black Moses to lead them out of the wilderness. He would lead them even if he never lived to see the Promised Land.

4 ‹‹‹‹‹‹‹‹‹‹‹‹‹‹‹‹‹

Black Man in White Europe

ON A HOT STILL NIGHT IN 1922 KENYATTA WENT TO YKA headquarters. Taking a Bible in his left hand and a lump of soil in his right, he swore a secret oath of allegiance to YKA.

The emergence of the YKA as the voice of the Kikuyu posed a sharp challenge to white power structure control of the tribe through "Uncle Toms" appointed as village chiefs. The white country squires, living in Edwardian elegance on their huge plantations, felt threatened by the militancy of the YKA. But they hesitated to suppress it out of fear of more riots like the Thuku demonstration.

That affair had provoked international protests, compelling the Colonial Office in London to insist in a 1923 British White Paper: "African interests must be paramount when in conflict with European and Indian interests."

Taking London at its word, Kenyatta spent much of his free time exhorting his fellow Kikuyu to join the YKA in the struggle against exploitation. Every day after work he would ride out to the African reserve, at first on a bike, later on a motorcycle. Everyone scampered out of the way of the big figure instantly recognizable by his large cowboy felt hat with beads-felt band, half-sleeve khaki jacket with four flap pockets, *kenyatta* fastened around his waist by a copper buckle, riding breeches and light brown boots.

He was too spectacular a figure to escape the observation of the district officer at Fort Hall, who reported darkly to his superiors in Nairobi, "That fellow Kenyatta is a dangerous agitator."

Kenyatta spoke for the YKA in presenting a petition to the governor at Fort Hall. He asked that coffee, which Africans were forbidden to grow because it was a cash crop that could make them independent of forced labor, be taken off the banned list. Other demands included self-government for the Kikuyu under their own chieftain; publication of Kenya's laws in the Kikuyu language; release of Harry Thuku; and the seating of a dozen elected Kikuyu representatives on the Legislative Council.

The governor disdained to recognize or discuss any of these grievances. YKA, he declared coldly, was no more than "an indeterminate collection of malcontents . . . with no constructive program of reform."

In 1925 the YKA was renamed the Kikuyu Central Association (KCA) to broaden its appeal for other central Kenya tribes, notably the Meru and Kamba.

That year the Church of Scotland Missions, which still ran the only schools and clinics for natives, sought to end the Kikuyu coming-of-age rites, which they opposed because of "certain barbarous practices involved." Church admission and the use of schools were denied to any Kikuyu parents who would not pledge to keep their children out of the rites.

At a meeting of KCA leaders, Kenyatta reacted with indignation. "First they take our lands," he charged, "and now they want to destroy our people's sacred customs!"

"But how can we go against the missionaries?" one KCA leader wondered. "We need every school and teacher if we're going to educate our young people. Certainly the government isn't going to build any schools for us!"

"Then why not build our own? And if the Christian Church for Europeans bars us, why not also build our own church?"

Agitated by the KCA, Kikuyu by the thousands began to boycott the Church of Scotland mission schools and churches. They contributed their labor and meager earnings to a new Kikuyu Independent Schools Association (KISA) and began building schools for their own children. KISA's plan called for a teachers' college to be built at Githunguri, with mission-educated Kikuyu as a faculty to train teachers for the new schools.

To the further dismay of the missionaries, many Kikuyu now rejected Christianity, returning to their ancient tribal religion. Some remained converted but set up their own pseudo-Christian sects—the Kikuyu African Orthodox Church, the Kikuyu Independent Pentecostal Church, and *Watu wa Mungu* (the People of God), which blamed the white man's airplanes for causing drought. Missionaries were outraged by the half-Christian, half-tribal rites that characterized these sects, considering them sacrilegious. They blamed Johnstone Kenyatta, most dynamic of the KCA leaders, for the schism.

He shrugged off their indignation. The fires of a new dream were beginning to warm his imagination. Once the Kikuyu had built all their own schools and churches, they could reorganize their shattered society into an all-black, anti-European power structure of their own.

What he needed now more than anything else was

time—time to hold off further encroachment by the white man while the KCA developed an army of educated, united Kikuyu to confront and eventually take over the reins of Kenya's government. Kenyatta's dream was a vision of independence.

In 1928 he was named general secretary of the KCA. The organization was now large enough to pay him a salary that let him leave government service and devote all his time to organizing the movement into a strong political force.

He began traveling around Kikuyuland, holding large meetings to explore tribal grievances, recruit members and raise money for KCA and KISA. In Nairobi he began a KCA newspaper in the Kikuyu language. *Muigwithania* was the first paper in that part of the world published by Africans.

To the indignation of the white settlers, Kenyatta dared publish antigovernment songs and inflammatory articles urging mass protests against the Crown Land Ordinance. If the Kikuyu got back their lands, he pointed out, the Europeans would not be able to get them to leave their villages as laborers without offering them decent pay, housing and working conditions. He made *Muigwithania* as hard-hitting as he could, knowing full well that the colonial government would not long tolerate its "subversive" ideas.

He was not surprised in 1929 when the white settlers led a legal attack to cripple the rapidly growing black nationalist movement. A Native Authority Ordinance forbade KCA organizers to collect money "without permits." Africans were forbidden to carry dangerous weapons, while Europeans were permitted to continue wearing sidearms.

No KCA meetings were allowed anywhere without

permission of the local chief, who was invariably a government-appointed stooge. KCA's president, Joseph Kangethe, defied this edict by holding unauthorized meetings. He was promptly arrested and sentenced to two years' imprisonment, leaving Kenyatta the leading spirit of the KCA movement.

The government then joined hands with the missionaries to ban KCA-sponsored district ceremonial dances as "indecent and seditious." Tribesmen found in possession of any ceremonial objects used on these occasions were prosecuted and punished for "witchcraft." Word reached Kenyatta in Nairobi that missionaries, aided by a government constabulary, had raided his native village of Ichaweri.

Among those who had been arrested and imprisoned for possessing such "works of the devil" was his own father, Ngengi. Ceremonial calabashes bequeathed to Ngengi by Kenyatta's grandfather Kongo, now dead, had been found in his hut. Kenyatta felt a choking fury at this insult to the memory of his beloved grandfather, even more than at the injustice done to his father.

The Indian population of Kenya, meanwhile, was also protesting its treatment by the white settlers. The Indians petitioned the Colonial Office in London for a new constitution that would give them representation on the Legislative Council. The Hilton Young Royal Commission arrived in 1928 to investigate. Kenyatta managed to win a hearing before it, and made a brilliant presentation of Kikuyu grievances.

Indian leaders of the colony observed that the commission seemed far more sympathetic to Kenyatta's cause then to their own. That gave one group of Indians with Communist connections an idea. They called on Kenyatta with an irresistible offer. Would he be willing to go to London to plead the case for a new constitution with the Secretary of State for the Colonies, if they paid all his expenses and supplied him with the legal help he needed?

There was no mystery about their motive. Whatever representation Kenyatta could win for natives in the government would also have to be given to the East Indians in Kenya. They were counting on his persuasive magnetism to appeal successfully to the London custodians of British justice.

He promptly accepted.

So in 1929 the big African in the cowboy felt hat sailed out of Mombasa for the great city whose pictures he had marveled at in the schoolbooks of the Church of Scotland Mission. First impressions of London overwhelmed the immigrant fresh from a rustic African colony.

He was staggered by the roar of traffic, the glamorous shops of Regent Street, the majesty of Admiralty Arch, the raising of the Tower Bridge, the booming chimes of Big Ben, the awesome majesty of Parliament, the flashing gaiety of Piccadilly Circus. So *this*, he reflected in awe, was the source of the white man's enormous power. No wonder the white settlers had swept aside the African's primitive civilization with such utter contempt!

He spent his first few weeks familiarizing himself with the fascinating city, studying Londoners and unconsciously imitating their manner of walking, talking and comporting themselves. In a little while he almost forgot that their skins were white and his was black, except when he caught glimpses of himself in store windows. He was fascinated to discover that the English at home, unlike the white settlers they had exported to Kenya, were remarkably indifferent to skin color. Sophisticated Londoners were used to visiting Asian and African diplomats from the outposts of the British Empire.

Kenyatta sought an interview with the Colonial Secretary, but he was unsuccessful because he lacked official credentials. He did, however, succeed in winning an invitation to testify before a House of Commons committee investigating the coming-of-age ceremonial rites complained of by the Church of Scotland Mission in Kenya.

Moving in awe through the solemn halls of Parliament, Kenyatta found himself stirred by reflections of the world power that for centuries had swirled through these same high corridors to which he, an African native, had now been summoned as part of an official hearing.

If only, he thought in mingled vanity and tenderness, *my mother could see her little Kamau now!*

The great dignity of the members gathered in the splendid committee room made him so nervous that he had to fight off a sense of panic. Hearing his voice boom out in the huge hall caused him to stammer. But as he realized from their expressions that they were not unsympathetic, his confidence returned and his voice grew steady. By the time he had finished explaining the importance of the coming-of-age rites to the Kikuyu, he had been persuasive enough to prevent a colonial government decree outlawing them.

While in Parliament he listened to some speeches delivered in Commons. He was deeply impressed. How brilliantly a British education taught white men to speak!

Despite his small success at the committee hearing, his real mission to London, he knew, had to be considered a failure. The Colonial Secretary's persistent refusal to see him amounted to rejection of Kikuyu grievances. He felt bitterly disillusioned. The British Home Office had saved face by issuing White Papers, theoretically acknowledging that native rights in the colonies should take precedence over the rights of white settlers.

This lip service to British justice maintained the respectability of colonialism and protected Britain's reputation as a world power. But in cold hard fact, while disapproving naked brutality by colonists, the Colonial Secretariat was largely, and conveniently, deaf to the grievances of the native populations under its control.

In his discouragement Kenyatta turned to the League Against Imperialism, a Communist group with London headquarters. Here he received an enthusiastic welcome as a leading spokesman for oppressed Africans. He was even given a quick trip to Moscow. To his astonishment, Kenyatta learned that Joseph Stalin envisioned a worldwide uprising of black people against white capitalism.

After London, Kenyatta found Moscow a vast but dreary city, with a language barrier that made him feel even more isolated. He was glad to leave for Germany, and he was welcomed in Berlin by Communists to whom he had been given introductions. He arrived to find the country in the throes of a struggle for power between the German Communist Party and Adolf Hitler's Nazi Party. The Weimar Republic was tottering and about to fall. The Berlin Reds sent Kenyatta to Hamburg as their delegate to a Communist-sponsored International Negro Workers' Congress.

His travels were giving him a European polish few Africans could boast, but achieving nothing for the Indians back home who had sponsored his mission to London. They tired of sending money without results, and in 1930 Kenyatta was compelled to return to Nairobi.

But what he had seen in Europe had opened his eyes to the possibility of a new and wonderfully different life. An ambitious, intelligent African, he was convinced, could go far in a country like England, and do more there for the cause of his people than he could back home. The *real* power to change things for the Kikuyu lay in London.

If he could stay there long enough, improving his education until his skill with words and arguments could match the white man's, sooner or later he would compel the Colonial Secretariat to recognize and deal with him. Like other Africans whose eyes had been opened to world realities, Kenyatta felt that the only effective training for African leadership lay in a European education.

Soon after his return he managed to obtain enough money, possibly from KCA funds, to take him back to London to testify before the Carter Kenya Land Commission, which was scheduled to leave for Nairobi in 1932 to investigate Kikuyu complaints.

Before his departure he was visited by leaders of the new Dini ya Jesu Kristo sect, one of the quasi-Christian churches splitting with the Church of Scotland. Shunning all foreign goods, they dressed in skins and carried forbidden weapons—bows and arrows. The government, spurred on by the missionaries, was harassing them with arrests and imprisonment. Kenyatta promised them he would inform the Colonial Secretariat about their persecution.

When he left for England late in 1931, he had no idea that it would be fifteen long years before he would see his beloved homeland again.

His first year was spent at a Quaker college in Woodbrooke, Selly Oak, where he studied and perfected his command of English. His life was like that of most poor students of the day—a dingy round of bed-sitting rooms, cheap cafés and radical politics.

He testified for the Kikuyu before the Carter Kenya Land Commission, which was scheduled to deliver its recommendations to the Colonial Secretariat in 1934. Determined to win the widest possible support for his tribe's grievances, he persisted in submitting petitions to the Colonial Office, writing letters to London papers and making soapbox speeches in Hyde Park and Trafalgar Square.

He was overjoyed at receiving a letter informing him that he had won an audience at the Colonial Secretariat. But the coolness of his reception made it perfectly plain that he was considered an upstart and a nuisance.

Chagrined, Kenyatta turned more and more to Communist friends, despite his skepticism about their motives in embracing him. Their axe to grind, he knew, was not justice for the Africans, but the use of Africans to help overthrow white capitalism and replace it by white communism. Nevertheless, he could see no other real hope or promise of aid for his fight against colonial injustice.

Leaving the Quaker school he moved to London, where he had made many friends among Negro intellectuals. Two of his closest companions were Kwame Nkrumah (later to become the President of Ghana and co-founder of the Pan-African Union movement) and Peter Abrahams, a noted South African writer. Another intimate friend was Paul Robeson, the massive, mighty-lunged American singer. For a while he shared the radical Robeson's flat near Charing Cross.

Robeson was appearing in a film version of Edgar Wallace's *Sanders of the River*. One day he asked Kenyatta how he would like to make some money as an actor. The threadbare African quickly agreed, and Robeson procured a role for him in the picture as a native African chief.

Hoping to pick up other film work, Kenyatta won permission to keep the chief's costume. He wore it to attract attention whenever he sought to publicize Kikuyu grievances. It helped make him a sought-after celebrity at London cocktail parties, leading to offers to lecture in costume.

His growing reputation brought an offer of a Soviet scholarship to study at the University of Moscow. He attended there between 1932 and 1934. Later the British government charged, on "reliable reports," that he had been a member of the London Communist Party and had studied revolutionary tactics at the Lenin School in Moscow.

They could offer no proof of these charges. Kenyatta's studies in Moscow were feeble evidence, because the Russians eagerly subsidized hundreds of bright African students at the University of Moscow, hoping to make converts of them.

If Kenyatta had, indeed, joined the Communist Party, or if he was simply an open-minded sympathizer, the record is nevertheless clear that shortly after his return from Moscow he dropped all of his Communist connections.

"I know about communism," he was to say thirty years later. "I've seen it, and cannot be fooled."

Back in England, he worked at the School of Oriental and African Studies as an assistant in phonetics, with enough time off to travel widely in Europe. He spent most of his time among anticolonial intellectuals of both races, including his old friend Mbui Koinange, who had gone to an American university to become the first Kikuyu to earn a degree.

While one part of Kenyatta deeply enjoyed the refinements of the white man's world, the other drew him back to his tribal origins. He eagerly read letters from home that kept him posted on developments in KCA's struggle.

At first KCA agitation had won a concession from the government. They could build their own schools—*if* they could find the land, money and teachers. But when KCA had shown that they could, the government angrily cracked down and forbade them to hold any more public meetings.

Clashes were mounting. In 1934 the Watu wa Mungu religious sect had been attacked by police in the Ndarugu Forest. Accused of mounting a rebellion, three members of the sect had been shot "accidentally." Kenyatta sensed dark days ahead for his people. The more threatened the white settlers felt, the more they would react with brutal measures against the Kikuyu.

Kenyatta knew that sooner or later he would have to choose between remaining in Europe, where a black man could live in freedom and equality, or returning home as a despised "African nigger" to take his place on the barricades.

The choice might be between life and death.

5 ‹‹‹‹‹‹‹‹‹‹‹‹‹‹‹‹‹‹‹‹‹

Kenyatta Comes Home

IN 1936 KENYATTA ATTENDED A POSTGRADUATE COURSE in anthropology at the London School of Economics and Political Science of the University of London. His sponsor was the brilliant Polish-born anthropologist, Professor Bronislaw Malinowski, famous for his studies of Southwest Pacific cultures. Impressed with Kenyatta's remarkable knowledge of Kikuyu tribal customs and lore, Malinowski arranged for his fees to be paid by the International Institute of African Languages and Culture.

It was Malinowski who encouraged a project Kenyatta had been mulling over for some time. Ever since he had come to Europe, Kenyatta had observed that most whites he met were fascinated by his accounts of African life. His memories of Kikuyu folklore were as fresh in his mind as when he had recited them in children's age-group competitions.

Why not write a whole book about them, explaining his African heritage to Europeans? It would help make the British realize why they were so tragically wrong in destroying this heritage with missionaries and colonialism. And it would enlist world sympathy for the Kikuyu cause.

"I'll call it *Facing Mount Kenya*," he told Mbui Koinange.

"It's a splendid idea," his American-educated friend agreed, "provided the KCA don't think you're getting too grand for them. An author and anthropologist—oh, my! I'm getting letters saying the elders feel we've been away from home so long, we've forgotten that we're Kikuyu."

Kenyatta deliberated. "I'll show them that we haven't. I won't even use my missionary name. I'll change Johnstone to something more Kikuyu, like Jomo. That's it, Jomo—'Burning Spear!' And if they want a picture of me for the book, I'll wear Kikuyu tribal dress."

The photograph he took for the cover of *Facing Mount Kenya* showed him draped in Koinange's robe of hydrox and blue monkey, one shoulder bare, enigmatically fingering the point of a spear they carved out of a wood plank.

Facing Mount Kenya explained the family group as the unifying factor in Kikuyu life, the source of all Kikuyu ideas about good and evil. It pointed out that the invasion of the white man, with his emphasis on people as individuals instead of family units, had disrupted Kikuyu society.

Writing with the perspective of years of study and travel in the European's world, Kenyatta urged Africans not to feel inferior to the white man. They should take pride in themselves, their tribes and their religion, he insisted, because their society was in many ways more admirable than the culture of the West.

Appearing in 1938, his book was a thunderbolt hurled at the white power structure in Kenya. One caustic reviewer labeled it "Kenyatta's Mein Kampf." Malinowski agreed with Kenyatta that it was tragically shortsighted simply to label educated African intellectuals as "agitators," as most white colonists did, and refuse to hear their appeals for a peaceful conciliation of differences.

By persistently ignoring African leaders like Kenyatta and treating their cause with contempt, Malinowski warned, "we drive them into the open arms of worldwide Bolshevism."

Facing Mount Kenya created a stir in academic circles, winning acclaim as the best anthropological study of a primitive people written from within. Jomo Kenyatta quickly found himself in great demand for lectures.

Despite his years of absence from his homeland, his reputation there as a KCA leader had not been forgotten. The international attention paid to his book now made him famous to additional millions of Africans as a leading world spokesman for the black cause of freedom and independence.

His education completed in a burst of literary brilliance, Kenyatta prepared to return home to pick up the reins of the KCA struggle where he had dropped them seven years earlier. But the outbreak of war with Germany at first delayed transportation, then made it out of the question.

Kenyatta made his contribution to the British war effort by taking a defense job as farm laborer in the Sussex village of Storrington at fourteen dollars a week. He enjoyed getting his hands back into rich soil once more, finding spiritual nourishment in direct contact with the earth.

At the same time he lectured on the Worker's Educational Association circuit, and worked on a second book called *My People of Kenya*, which appeared in 1942. Through the lecture bureau he met a white woman lecturer named Edna Grace Clark, who taught school in the neighborhood.

A quiet, radical teacher free of prejudice, she fell in

love with the charming and brilliant African. They were married in 1943. It did not disturb Kenyatta that he still had two African wives in Kenya, since in his private life he followed Kikuyu, not European, law. He and Edna lived quietly in Storrington, and she bore him a son named Peter.

Kenyatta was enormously popular in the village, his good nature and bulk winning him the affectionate nickname "Jumbo"—a pun on Jomo—at the local pub, the White Horse Inn.

"When I knew him during those years," wrote a Storrington lady many years later, "his eyes were usually alight with laughter rather than afire with zeal."

But even during this idyllic time he never lost his fervor for the Kikuyu cause. He grew progressively more depressed at news from Mbui Koinange, who had returned to Kenya just before the outbreak of war. More and more Kikuyu were being removed from their villages onto the reserves. The colonial government had used the war as a pretext for banning the KCA and all other native political associations. The KCA had gone underground, operating clandestinely.

Kenyatta kept up his contacts with white friends in Britain's Labor Party, hoping that if Labor came to power after the war he could count on them to help sweep away the repressive colonial structure in Kenya.

In 1944 he began to detect the winds of change blowing in the letters of Koinange. Harry Thuku, released from prison, had joined with another Kikuyu "troublemaker," James Gichuru, in forming a new "educational" organization—Kenya African Study Union (KASU). The government suspected, correctly, that the real purpose of KASU was to organize a broad nationalist movement for freedom.

The Crown moved swiftly to handcuff KASU and

dampen rising native discontent by making its first appointment of an African to the Legislative Council to "represent" native interests. He was Eliud Mathu, one of KASU's more moderate leaders. Koinange had bid for the post, but the Crown felt that Mathu would be easier to control and ignore.

Kenyatta was not taken in. Writing a pamphlet called *Kenya: Land of Conflict,* he warned the colonial government that if it did not show real flexibility in responding to African grievances, a black revolution might be necessary.

As soon as the war was over, Thuku, Gichuru, Mathu, Koinange and others sent Kenyatta money for his passage, urging him to come home at once and lead KASU's struggle for independence. Gichuru, president of KASU, promised that this office would be his when he returned to Kenya.

But the celebrated expatriate who had been so eager to return before the war, and who had so long fought for his people's cause from a distance of three thousand miles, now hesitated. White England had accepted him; would white Kenya?

Although he had earned a university degree in America, Koinange had found no open door in white society when he returned to Kenya, and had been offered only third-rate jobs available to Europeans with just an elementary education.

For a proud, ambitious, sophisticated African like Kenyatta, who for so many years now had moved in cultured European circles, a return to the humiliation of life on the bleak reserves or in Nairobi's slums was hardly an enticing prospect. Moreover, he assured himself, he could do more good for his people in the free air of London than under the thumbs of the white settlers of Kenya.

He was involved, for one thing, in organizing a Pan-African Foundation with Kwame Nkrumah and other African leaders to try to unite Africans of all British colonies in one great independence movement. Nkrumah wanted it to begin as an inner-core secret society, suggesting that each of the leaders spill a few drops of his blood into a bowl of wine to be drained by all with a secret oath of brotherhood.

"Kenyatta laughed at the idea," revealed South African leader Peter Abrahams. "He conceived of our struggle in modern twentieth-century terms with no ritualistic blood nonsense. In the end Nkrumah drifted away from us. We were too tame and slow for him."

Twice his friends back home sent money for him to return; twice he hesitated. But then two things happened to convince him that he must go. A left-wing Pan-African Congress he helped Nkrumah organize in Manchester failed miserably. The chains of colonialism, he now felt, could never be struck off Africa from without, but only from within.

Then KASU dropped the word "Study" from its name, calling itself simply the Kenya African Union (KAU). Kenyatta was impressed that the movement was now strong and dynamic enough to proclaim bluntly that its true aim was not simply education but militant black nationalism.

Once he had made up his mind to return, he was filled with nostalgia at the vision of the green hills of Kenya, his home. He thought of taking his white wife Edna and their son Peter back with him, but decided against it. The color bar in Kenya would make their life intolerable. There would be nowhere they could live together peacefully as they did in England.

Besides, he knew there was bloodshed ahead. The white settlers would not give up their stranglehold on

Kenya without a bloody struggle. And Peter, now three, would have a far better chance of receiving a good education in England than in a black colony torn by turmoil.

So in September, 1946, he took leave of his third wife and his son, returning to the homeland he had left fifteen years before. Kenya was now a land of 30,000 whites, 19,000 East Indians and 5,500,000 Africans. Kenyatta's entry into the port of Mombasa and his railroad trip inland to Nairobi, both now postwar boomtowns, left him with mixed sensations.

It was no simple matter for him to stop feeling like a European citizen of the mother country and begin feeling again like a tribal Kikuyu and black native of Kenya.

"Places like London and Manchester," he later recalled ruefully, "I knew better than Nairobi now."

But the die was cast.

Jomo Kenyatta, now fifty-six, had come home at last.

He received a hero's welcome. On all sides tremendous crowds of Africans cheered and fought to touch the legendary, highly educated black man who had been treated with respect as an equal by whites all over Europe; who had informed the world about the injustices they had suffered; who had now come home to rescue them from their bondage.

Wherever he went, his huge bearded figure was instantly recognized. Hundreds, then thousands, of native voices would cry out the magic name that excited the nation: *"Jomo! Jomo Kenyatta!"* All of Kenya echoed to its thunder.

He was amazed, delighted and deeply stirred.

The fifteen-year absence that had made him a legend, he discovered, had also wrought other great changes in his country. The war had brought boom times for white farmers, who had received high prices for crops supplied to the military, and for white businessmen, whose prosperity was evident in the new international airport at Nairobi and the expansion of Mombasa as a bustling international seaport. Kenyatta hardly recognized Nairobi now for its skyscrapers, beautiful wide avenues and wealthy villas. The boom reflected huge investments by overseas banks, oil firms and export houses.

But the condition of his own people, he noted grimly, was even more wretched and depressing than when he had left. The government had spent all its money to benefit only the white power structure. On the reserves and in the ghetto slums there were only poverty and hardship.

The reserves were shockingly overcrowded, not only because the white settlers had grabbed more African land, but also because of a population explosion among the Kikuyu. There were two main reasons, and ironically missionary interference could be blamed for both. Youth was running wild, no longer restrained by tribal elders, whose authority had been undermined by church attacks on Kikuyu family life.

In addition to a great upsurge of pregnancies among the unwed, the Kikuyu death rate had been sharply cut by inroads made by missionary medicine on witch doctors' practice.

Both developments made the tribal need for land more urgent than ever. KAU agitators intensified popular anger over "the stolen lands," and spread the defiant slogan, "Africa for the Africans!"

Kenyatta found more dynamite ready to be touched off in the disillusionment of native veterans who had volunteered for the King's Africa Rifles during the war. Many had served abroad with distinction. Like himself, they had become aware of anticolonial movements overseas and of countries where white men treated them with dignity. They had held meaningful army jobs, and had been taught such skills as driving and communications.

But then they had returned home to face a choice of either unemployment or menial jobs as servants at low wages. They were expected to resume their old segregated lives in ghetto shanties or on reserves and to submit to being treated with contempt by the white man, flogged whenever he chose.

Many moved to the cities and joined a growing street army of toughs, thugs and criminals, utilizing their military training to steal a livelihood rather than work as laborers for $5.60 a month.

Postwar frustration and bitterness had grown rapidly among all the African tribes of Kenya, but most of all among the Kikuyu, who had suffered more than any other. Rumors spread that Kikuyu war veterans who had turned criminal were joining the suppressed KCA, still operating underground. On still, clear nights an ominous throb of tribal drums rose from the dense forests of Kikuyuland, striking apprehension into the hearts of uneasy Europeans who heard them.

These, then, were the conditions Kenyatta found when he began his crusade to unite all Kenya tribes in KAU. When he called his first meeting at Njoro, thousands of villagers came from all over the Rift Valley on foot, in carts and on old buses to hear the words of wisdom of the great Kikuyu leader back from London. Many wondered if they would be able to understand the returned patriot. After so many years away, would he still remember how to speak in Kikuyu or Swahili?

A babble of high excitement and anticipation filled the crisp sunny air. The huge mob gathered around the speaker's stand on a grassy plain grew increasingly restless as several speakers wasted time with unnecessary introductions. Then finally, to a great roar of delight, a heavyset man in a brown leather jacket mounted the platform.

Holding aloft his carved walking stick, he boomed out an emotional greeting of *"Eeeeeeeeaaaahh!"* It was a barrel-chested shout of pure joy to be back among his people. They understood and responded with wild applause and laughter.

An intensely magnetic speaker with flamboyant, dramatic gestures, he had a hypnotic effect upon his vast audience. He spoke to them in Swahili mixed with Kikuyu phrases, to remind other tribes that he was now a spokesman for *all* Africans, as well as to prove to Kikuyu elders that he had not forgotten the tribal tongue of his people.

He told them of his accomplishments for them in England, then spoke of the future of Kenya. "I do not want the Europeans to leave the country," he declared, "but it is time they started to behave like guests in our house. They came to us as strangers, and we gave them hospitality, and then they claimed that the house belonged to them."

He smiled at the deafening roar of approval. "We carried their women on our shoulders and drew them in rickshaws from Mombasa to Nairobi, so that their legs should not tire walking through the scrub and forests of thorn. We sent our young men to sacrifice their lives to help the British fight and conquer Germany. The white officers were rewarded with farms on which to settle in our land, and loans with which to stock them. Our African soldiers were rewarded with the color bar and unemployment, although there had been no color bar to prevent our dying for Britain in the war!"

His eloquent oratory held the vast crowd transfixed in awed silence, the spell broken only to laugh at the force and sting of his caustic wit, or to sway and chant with him in mock hymns praising KAU. The thousands who heard him thrilled at the daring things he said, because all knew that listening in the crowd were native spies who would report every defiant word to the colonial government.

"We must unite together in KAU and forget tribalism," he urged. "We must not let the Europeans forget that the land they tread is ours. We should work hard, and try to educate our people as well as quickly as possible, so that they can take over the government of the country for us!"

When he finished, thousands of African women among his listeners gave him five trilling cries—the *ngemi* reserved for the birth of a male child and in honor of a great leader. The enthusiastic crowd lingered in excited groups, reluctant to shake off the magic spell he had cast.

For the first time since the white man had come to Kenya, they were powerfully agitated by a strange new emotion.

Hope!

6 ◄◄◄◄◄◄◄◄◄◄◄◄◄◄◄◄◄◄◄

Mau Mau!

IF KENYATTA HAD HAD ANY DOUBTS ABOUT THE WISDOM of returning from England, he had none now. He was exhilarated by the thrill of power that came from swaying vast crowds, from being worshipped as a demigod, from knowing that his people would follow blindly wherever he led—into revolution or massacre or election halls. His responsibility filled him with awe.

As many as 40,000 Africans at a time flocked to hear him. Women especially idolized him. Although he visited both his African families, he did not rejoin either. Instead a pretty young Kikuyu woman named Ngina became his favorite and most cherished wife, by whom he eventually had four children. His devotion to the shy and worshipful Ngina became legendary.

They lived in a new home built for him in Ichaweri. Above it he flew the flag of KAU—black for Africa, red to show that African blood was the same as the white man's, green for the fertility of Kenya's highlands. Whenever he could be at home, he loved to spend his leisure weeding his vegetable gardens, reading Nietzsche and Schopenhauer, and fascinating children with the old Kikuyu legends.

He knew he was on a collision course with the white

power structure in Kenya. All that saved him from arrest was the Europeans' fear of touching off a black revolution. But he also knew that they could not afford to let him go on organizing insurrection. He sought a peaceful solution by appealing to the government to agree to gradual reforms.

He told the governor, Sir Philip Mitchell, that he was prepared to participate in the Legislative Council as spokesman for KAU. Mitchell, baffled, sought advice from the white settlers, who regarded the "Kukes" (Kikuyu) as "just fifty years out of the trees." Then he summoned Kenyatta.

"Now, Mr. Kenyatta, you have been away so long, you are almost like a foreigner. You must stay here for one or two years in order to adapt yourself to the country." He added arrogantly that if Kenyatta wished to enter politics, he should begin at the bottom by seeking election to the local Native Council of his area. Kenyatta suppressed his anger.

"Now that the war is over," he said, "I can't see any reason why the ban on KCA can't be lifted."

Mitchell's nostrils flared in aristocratic affront.

"KCA's leaders must remain in jail for misbehavior!"

Mbui Koinange, who had been completing the building of the Kenya Teachers' College at Githunguri, told him, "Jomo, the white settlers are too scared to yield an inch. They hear the tom-toms all over Africa, and they're desperate."

"They're bloody fools," Kenyatta growled. "They can save their necks and the system if they'll work with moderates like us and agree to reforms. If they don't, our people will get disgusted and turn to the witch doctors and the criminals running the KCA. If Mitchell waits until that happens to turn to us, it will be too late!"

This realization apparently began to dawn on Governor Mitchell, because in March, 1947, he appointed Kenyatta to the African Land Settlement and Utilization Board. Hopeful, Kenyatta attended every meeting over the next two years. But he soon found that the government was deaf to his views, none of which were allowed to influence the status quo.

"I am being encouraged to bark in private," he told Koinange sarcastically, "so that I won't bite in public!"

In May, 1947, Koinange turned over to him control of the independent Kenya Teachers' Training College at Githunguri, as well as the Kikuyu Independent Schools Association. The new school system was already promulgating Kenyatta's credo that the African had a more admirable way of life than the European. Teachers led pupils in reciting a new pledge: "I believe in God, the Father Almighty, in the leadership of Jomo Kenyatta, and the righteous complaints and unity of the Kikuyu."

Like most African leaders, Kenyatta placed no great store by modesty, and saw only political advantage in letting himself be exalted. Glorification was more than simply balm for early years of humiliation as a black man in a white society. For Jomo Kenyatta it was primarily a political weapon—a unifying force to put worshipful Africans behind him in an almost-religious crusade for freedom.

He worried about the new African schools developed by KISA. They were woefully understaffed because Githunguri College could not turn out trained teachers fast enough. Inadequate as they were, however, he did not underestimate the great sacrifices Kikuyu made to build and support them.

Sometimes they gave half their cash income and sold their land and cattle to make contributions. Whole communities had carried stones to hilltops, working like bees building precious hives. The children themselves had helped put up roofs, the work becoming part of their education even before they could formally become students.

Under KISA the Kikuyu managed to build 300 schools to educate 60,000 children. When a school was built, ragged children, many in cutdown versions of their fathers' old army uniforms, would pore over their books studiously, even when unmonitored. Hungry to learn, they would carry home the day's lessons to teach their parents at night.

Jomo Kenyatta's heart swelled with pride and joy at the determination of his people to learn their way to freedom.

The reaction of the white settlers to this educational ferment was sullen. An American reporter for *The Nation* asked why, if the government really had the welfare of Africans at heart as it claimed, it did not assist Kenyatta in one of the greatest educational movements of history.

"False shepherds, false shepherds!" snapped a legislator, shaking his head. "These people are sadly exploited by their own leaders. In any event, Rome was not built in a day. We *do* have their welfare at heart. Just let us have a few hundred years more!"

Jomo Kenyatta, now fifty-seven, could not wait that long.

In June, 1947, James Gichuru stepped down as president of KAU and Kenyatta was unanimously acclaimed in his place. A comfortable house was built for him at Githunguri, facing Mount Kenya. Now he was wearing two hats of African power simultaneously, and he began using one to augment the other.

Political indoctrination of teachers at the Training College spread KAU nationalism through the Kikuyu Independent Schools system. And the KAU organization galvanized support for the schools, to provide the army of educated Africans needed to win and operate an independent Kenya.

Kenyatta's thorniest problem was the fear of Kikuyu domination by Kenya's other tribes. Some of them were hesitantly won over by his assurances that he was fighting for a coalition African government, not a Kikuyu autocracy. KAU grew steadily until it had 100,000 members.

New thousands rushed to KAU's banners when Kenyatta demanded that the white settlers stop cutting down sacred trees indiscriminately in clearing farmland. This offense to the gods, he charged, had produced drought in Kenya.

"I myself remember pools in which a full grown man could get out of his depth," he told crowds, "and in which we all used to bathe, but which are now replaced by dry soil!"

Most KAU leaders stood in awe of his tremendous impact upon the Kenyan masses, but a few privately grumbled that he was building a personality cult based on his charm and magnetism, rather than a solid following for KAU.

"I'm not sure he's a good leader," one insisted. "He collects much money, but we see no records of it. He lives much better than we do. If we ask him a direct question, he knows how to evade it. If we say he is avoiding an answer, he laughs and makes us feel foolish. Oh, he is clever and intelligent enough! And he has made Africans want education above all else, which is wise. But he is also a master actor. Maybe he has been acting for too long!"

Impervious to his critics, Kenyatta escalated his struggle with the colonial government in July, 1947, by bringing about a series of strikes. A large KAU meeting he called at Fort Hall resulted in a mass refusal by

Kikuyu women to work on a government land-terracing project.

In September a native worker in the Uplands Bacon Factory refused to contribute to Kenyatta's fund-raising drive for Githunguri College. The other workers demanded that he be fired. Management refused, and they struck. The district commissioner called out the police. In the riot that followed, the police opened fire, killing three workers, wounding six others. Scores were dragged off to jail.

In Mombasa that month a second strike, also suppressed by brutal police tactics, made it clear to the colonial government that Jomo Kenyatta had begun challenging their economic dictatorship over the lives of African workers.

Colonel Meinertzhagen, who had warned the white settlers against their harsh policies forty-five years earlier, grew deeply concerned. He discussed the soaring unrest with a Kikuyu chief he knew and trusted. Then, alarmed, he sent an urgent letter of warning to Government House:

"The chief fears an outbreak of violence against Europeans involving murders on a large scale under the direction of a secret society now in existence called 'Maw Maw' [sic] whose influence in the tribe is growing. . . . I may add that I believe this chief and do not consider his warning exaggerated." Meinertzhagen urged conciliation of KAU by compromises on at least some of its complaints.

Governor Mitchell shrugged off the warning disdainfully. He read a second communication in his mail with equal contempt. It was another letter from KAU full of demands.

Kenyatta demanded that all African citizens be enrolled as voters. All laws discriminating against colored people must be revoked. All Highland farms taken from the Kikuyu must be restored. Representation in the Legislative Council, which even now had only four African members, must be increased realistically. "It is absurd," Kenyatta protested, "to have just four Africans representing the majority of 5,500,000, while the tiny white minority of 30,000 Europeans are given *eleven* representatives!"

Mitchell flung the letter into his wastebasket.

With that gesture went the last hope of reconciliation between black and white in Kenya. What Mitchell did not know was that the danger warned of by Meinertzhagen was genuine, serious and growing by the hour. Only concessions to Kenyatta could have averted the impending catastrophe.

By refusing to agree to any constitutional reforms, the governor had doomed the white society of Kenya, and those Africans who supported it, to a ghastly reign of terror.

Mau Mau!

There were many confused reports about this cult —what it was, who led it, what it meant, the atrocities it was rumored to encourage. Some thought it had begun with the Dini ya Jesu Kristo cult, who prayed facing Mount Kenya, wore skins, carried bows and arrows and uttered lionlike roars sounding like *Mau Mau*. Others said the name was secret Kikuyu slang for "I will eat you up." Those who have sought clues as to the real origin of *Mau Mau* seem, inexplicably, to have overlooked the most likely explanation of all.

The hard core of Mau Mau was a Kikuyu organization called the Forty Group, because they had gone through their coming-of-age rites together in 1940. Having served in the Army, most had drifted afterward into the unemployment of Nairobi, where they had mixed politics with burglary and thuggery. Early in September, 1947, they became the Kikuyu Maranga African Union (KMAU), with two thousand members.

Dropping the tribal designation, the initials spelled MAU—obviously more than a striking coincidence.

The Forty Group had joined forces with veteran KCA leaders operating underground, and KMAU was transformed into a new version of the still-forbidden KCA. Members swore secret oaths that varied in ferocity, depending upon branch leaders. Many swore to terrify the white man out of Kenya, and drive those who remained into the sea.

The earliest oaths seem simply to have been pledges of unity and brotherhood in a struggle for land and freedom. Gradually, however, the nature of the oaths changed as the criminal element turned Mau Mau into a terrorist organization with dreadful ceremonies and savage warfare.

Over sacrifices of sheep and goats many Mau Mau recruits swore, "I must kill my brother if ordered, or may this oath kill me. I must hate my father and mother, or may this oath kill me. I must steal firearms when ordered. I must not lift a hand against any Mau Mau, but I must kill any Kikuyu if so ordered. When the red-buck horn is blown, if I leave a European farm without killing the owner, may this oath kill me. I swear to tell no one of this oath."

Some oathing ceremonies even involved cannibalism and other depravities. They usually took place in the forests of Kikuyuland at midnight, with recruits swearing the oath as they faced Mount Kenya. Fearful that the god Ngai would destroy them if they violated their oaths, they obeyed orders to kill members of their own families and clans unsympathetic to Mau Mau, and often endured excruciating torture when captured rather than reveal Mau Mau secrets.

While many joined the Mau Mau out of hatred of the white man, others took the oath because of threats to murder them by horrible dismemberment. One Colonial Office estimate put the total number of Kikuyu who had taken the oath at 90 percent of the tribe.

Although Jomo Kenyatta preferred to profess ignorance of Mau Mau, there is no question that he well knew the extent of the terrorist movement. What is not clear is whether he felt powerless as the head of KAU to restrain the hotheads in the illegal KCA, or whether he secretly approved of Mau Mau as a violent ally in the struggle against colonialism. Perhaps he felt that the white settlers, faced with the horrors of Mau Mau, would turn to him and to KAU in desperation to save them.

In any event, African political activity in Kenya polarized at two centers—the legal KAU organization at Githunguri, with charismatic Jomo Kenyatta as its popular leader; and the clandestine, conspiratorial Mau Mau led by KCA nationalists and the Forty Group of young thugs.

However much Kenyatta may have genuinely deplored the violence of Mau Mau—*if* he did—he could not help but know that many of its practitioners also held minor offices in the middle and lower echelons of KAU. But even if he knew who they were, it would have been dangerous for him to remove or denounce them. Mau Mau leaders could tolerate the African idol Kenyatta who looked the other way, but never a Kenyatta who fought them.

Two important leaders of the Forty Group, with whom Kenyatta had worked before the war when KCA was legal, were Joseph Kangethe and Jesse Kariuki.

Worried that he might go over to the government side if he were taken into the Legislative Council, they proposed forcing him to take a Mau Mau oath. Other KCA leaders argued that this was unnecessary.

They were already using his name without authority. Thousands of Kikuyu had joined the Mau Mau under the impression that they were doing what Kenyatta wanted. Let Jomo stand above the storm, if he preferred, as long as KCA could claim him as its sub rosa patron saint!

Angry at this tactic, Kenyatta wrote a terse letter in 1948 summoning all KCA leaders to a conference. He was determined to thrash out the whole question of leadership of the Kenya freedom movement, and insist that KCA dissolve its clandestine activities and work legally within the framework of KAU. Second thoughts of either fear, caution or indecision, however, caused him not to send the letter.

It remained in his files until government police found it there four years later, interpreting it as proof of Kenyatta's link with the illegal KCA leaders. The government also had other reasons for regarding him as the moving spirit behind Mau Mau.

In its pagan oathing ceremonies, Mau Mau used oaths and hymns which were burlesques of Christian sacraments, with the name of Kenyatta substituted for Jesus. The government felt sure that the initials of the pseudo-Christian sect calling itself Dini ya J.K. did not stand for Jesu Kristo but Jomo Kenyatta.

Mau Mau found fertile soil in the decaying tribal system. It capitalized on the misery and spiritual insecurity of the dispossessed Kikuyu. By 1948 one million Kikuyu had been forced onto reserves originally intended for three hundred thousand. Mau Mau appealed to their ancient traditions of secrecy, to oaths that bound them together, to belief in the great power of those oaths. It gave them a new, reassuring discipline to replace the old tribal controls that had largely disappeared because of European disruption.

All through 1948 Kikuyu from the reserves and Kikuyu farm labor in the Highlands flocked to the forests to join mass oathing ceremonies. Settlers, missionaries and district officials made frantic complaints to the government.

"There is a rumor circulating," the Fort Hall district commissioner warned, "that all the wrongs of the Kikuyu will be simultaneously righted by the murder of all Europeans." He reported great difficulty in getting any natives, even children, to say a word about the mysterious Mau Mau cult.

While the Mau Mau took the route of terror to end white colonialism in Kenya, Jomo Kenyatta competed for the allegiance of his people through a determined program of education, self-improvement and political struggle.

But increasingly it became clear that his pleas for reason and peaceful change were being drowned out by the rising bedlam of clashes between black and white madmen.

7 <<<<<<<<<<<<<<<<<<<<<<

"Mau Mau! What Is That?"

KENYATTA WAS NO DEMAGOGUE. HE DID NOT TELL VAST crowds only what they wanted to hear. He boldly scolded them for their own faults, insisting that they must not blame the Europeans for *all* their troubles. He deplored embezzlement by black officials, declining Kikuyu morality on the reserves and in the city slums, dishonest dealing by African traders.

He had finally forced the government to permit Africans to plant cash crops—tea and coffee. Why, he demanded, were so few taking this chance to free themselves from the need to work for the white settlers? Why also weren't African farmers using modern soil conservation methods?

But neither did he spare the white settlers.

"Kenya would be a paradise," he told an audience at Meru in August, 1948, "if the Europeans went back where they came from. Don't think I don't like the English. I *do* like them—in England. Where they soon all will be!"

Indignant white settlers demanded that Jomo Kenyatta be deported for sedition and treason. If the government refused to act, they threatened, they would take matters into their own hands. There was no doubt in their minds that *he* was the mastermind behind Mau Mau. Why, just look at the picture of the scoundrel in his book—posing in animal skins, fingering a spear and looking sinister! And what about the title, *Facing Mount Kenya?* For oathing, of course!

But the government hesitated. Arresting so revered a figure as Jomo Kenyatta could touch off a black revolution. He also had great influence among the liberals, intellectuals and Labor Party in England. Any move against him would unquestionably provoke a blast from the Colonial Home Office demanding to know what the devil the governor thought he was doing. So the burly, bearded KAU leader continued to travel freely around Kenya, acclaimed at the first glimpse of his open-necked colored shirt and elephant-headed walking stick. No other African could match his charisma.

He repeatedly warned the government and the white settlers to accept interracial cooperation before it was too late. Some Europeans, reading the Mau Mau handwriting on the wall, prudently formed the Kenya Citizens' Association to support Kenyatta's demand for a real voice by KAU in the Legislative Council. But time was running out. During the summer of 1950 a number of Kikuyu who refused to take the Mau Mau oath were brutally murdered.

One non-Kikuyu leader of KAU, Tom Mbotela, denounced these atrocities and urged Kenyatta to join him in this condemnation. Kenyatta hesitated. He deplored the atrocities as much as Mbotela—he was too much of a civilized European not to. But he was also playing for high stakes—Kenyan independence. Mau Mau, however savage, was a force for freedom and one that supported his struggle. What encouragement, in contrast, had the government given his demands for African justice and representative government?

However, when he, Koinange and Mbotela met with the white Kenya Citizens' Association, he told chairman Sir Charles Mortimer that KAU opposed Mau Mau tactics.

"Very well," Mortimer said. "Then prove it to the government and all of the Europeans in Kenya. Call a mass meeting, Mr. Kenyatta, and denounce Mau Mau openly!"

Kenyatta reflected, his eyes inscrutable as he stroked his graying beard. "All right, I'll do it! But first I want a *quid pro quo*. Let the government come out openly in agreement with our demands for political reforms!"

The Kenya Citizens' Association urged the governor to give Kenyatta a sign of flexibility. But the governor was under increasing pressure from the white settlers. He feared further that any concession to Kenyatta would discourage those Kikuyu who were defying the Mau Mau and reporting threats to the police. Their cooperation was indispensable.

Pressed by the outraged white settlers, who estimated that Mau Mau membership had grown to a frightening 200,000, the government outlawed the movement on August 12, 1950. Heavy punishment was decreed for all convicted of giving or taking the oath. In the next six months, over 150 Kikuyu were arrested as violators.

Three weeks after the governor had banned Mau Mau, he dropped a bombshell in the ranks of KAU by suppressing the Kikuyu Independent Schools Association (KISA) because of its "connection with Mau Mau." Kenyatta protested indignantly. Was *this* the cooperation the Kenya Citizens' Association had promised—the road to racial reconciliation?

Sir Charles Mortimer shrugged. "You can't really blame the government, you know," he pointed out. "You still haven't spoken out against Mau Mau. When you do, perhaps the ban on KISA will be lifted!"

Kenyatta brooded. But while he debated with himself in Hamlet-like indecision, the Forty Group moved swiftly to terrorize informers. Those who testified for the government in anti-Mau Mau trials were found floating in the Ruiru River, horribly mutilated. Mau Mau recruiters were ordered to inflict torture and death on any African who witnessed an oathing and refused to join, or who was sent on a Mau Mau errand which he failed to complete, for any reason.

"You know you could stop it if you really wanted to," Sir Mortimer challenged Kenyatta. "Your word is law among your people. When you told them to boycott British beer, they stopped drinking British beer. When you told them to stop wearing British hats, they did. Tell them to stop taking or obeying Mau Mau oaths—and they will stop!"

Kenyatta replied coolly, "I have yet to see any signs of accommodation on the part of the government to our legitimate demands. However, I will see what I can do."

On February, 1951, an enormous gathering of 30,000 Africans crowded into a KAU meeting called in a field outside Nairobi. They roared their devotion to the heavy-set, bearded African in leather jacket and tribal cap when he flicked a fly-whisk over his shoulder and shouted, *"Uhuru!"*—the Swahili word for freedom.

He told them that KAU was making progress in getting the Europeans to agree to concessions correcting the injustices against Africans. Suddenly a Kikuyu defector in the pay of the government shouted a prearranged challenge: "Tell us where you stand on Mau Mau, Kenyatta!"

He smiled and looked around roguishly.

"Mau Mau?" he asked in mock innocence. "What is that?" The crowd roared with laughter, and his eyes twinkled. *"Ndui, ndui, Mau Mau!"* ("I haven't the faintest idea of what Mau Mau is all about!") He added, "I don't even know what language it is, and I know quite a few African languages!"

He finished off his speech with a few sly antigovernment jokes told in long, low chuckles, then beamed at the delighted ovation of the crowd. Afterward Harry Thuku hugged him enthusiastically, grinning, "Jomo, you really should have been a comedian in the theater!"

But moderate Kikuyu chiefs in KAU were deeply worried. Alarmed by the wholesale desertion of their people to the Mau Mau, they urged Kenyatta to stop the trend in an important speech to the Kiambu district. So before an enormous crowd estimated to be 50,000, he called upon the assembled Kikuyu to "put a public curse" upon Mau Mau.

"All those people who agree we should get rid of Mau Mau, put up your hands," he shouted. Thousands of hands rose. After a thoughtful pause, he led them in reciting an enigmatic tribal imprecation: "Let Mau Mau disappear—down to the roots of the Mikongoe tree underneath the ground!"

The Mikongoe tree was a mythical tree in Kikuyu legend, signifying the unknown. When Kenyatta's words were reported to the white settlers, they interpreted his "curse" as a subtle signal to the Mau Mau to go underground and work there in secret for revolution. They noted angrily, too, that whenever Kenyatta made even mild references to Mau Mau practices as evil, he would convulse his listeners by pausing and suggesting dryly, "Now let us take a little tobacco."

The settlers construed that to mean, "Take what I

have just said with a pinch of salt." They were convinced that he was not opposing Mau Mau but mocking opposition to it. Why else did the Mau Mau continue to adulate him as an African messiah in their parodies of Christian hymns?

The white settlers were bitterly convinced that the perversion of the Christian liturgy was being used to give spiritual power to the Mau Mau by capitalizing on the confused faith of the lapsed African Christian. They warned the government that Kenya would be plunged "back into the abyss of primitive and debased tribalism" unless it immediately arrested that "evil-eyed, hard-drinking, wenching, bloody-minded terrorist"—Jomo "Burning Spear" Kenyatta.

Governor Mitchell still hesitated. Apart from his fear of touching off a revolution, he knew that the Crown would have a difficult time proving any connection between the enigmatic Jomo Kenyatta and Mau Mau. It might be shown that he had done nothing to stop it, but that was no punishable crime. It was something else again to prove that he was the secret mastermind of the terrorists.

The government had new evidence that some lower-echelon KAU officials had used oaths to sign up new members, but these were only the usual tribal oaths used to cement unity among Kikuyu, Embu, Meru and other tribes. They soothed a common Kikuyu fear of being killed by sorcery, binding different tribes together with a mutual vow that one would not invoke magic spells against the other.

There was no evidence to link Kenyatta to the bestial oaths of some Mau Mau groups. In fact, the frequency of such bloodthirsty ceremonies may have been exaggerated by alarmed white colonials. "To imply that these sorts of oaths were indulged in wholesale by most of the Kikuyu tribe," declared one Mau Mau member, "is like saying that all Englishmen are child-rapers and murderers simply because a few Englishmen do this every year."

As time passed and the colonial government showed no inclination to recognize KAU as the voice of the Kenya African, Jomo Kenyatta's mood grew increasingly grim.

In 1952 the government tried a new ploy. A sprinkling of seats in a new Legislative Council was given to a few African politicians willing to "play the game." Kenyatta countered with a caustic announcement that KAU did not recognize such token representation by government supporters as a genuine African participation in the Council.

Continuing to barnstorm around the country, he spoke at enormous rallies to which people streamed on foot from miles around. The tone of his talks grew sharper, stirring a restless anger among his masses of listeners.

"The land is ours," he told a crowd of 30,000 at Thika. "When the Europeans came, they kept us back and took our land. We want self-government. *Don't be afraid to spill your blood to get the land!*" Great roars of approval sent chills of apprehension down the spines of white settlers.

The overseas press began to speculate about revolution. Robert Ruark, American author of the novel *Uhuru!*, claimed to have a document proving that the Mau Mau were an "African Communist unit." Kenya's white settlers immediately demanded an investigation of the source of KAU funds.

The calmer London *Times* reported, "There has been some outside help in the form of advice and assistance by Indians and Europeans, both in Kenya and beyond . . . [but] there is no evidence whatever of 'Moscow intervention.' "

A *Nation* reporter interviewed one of Kenyatta's followers to determine the extent to which his disciples had been trained in Communist ideology. What did he know about Moscow?

"It welcomed Jomo Kenyatta," was the reply. "It said he was as good as the Europeans. It was the first European city to do that." Had he ever heard of Communism? "Yes . . . it is something European, I think. We can't bother about European things. We have to think about the Kikuyu."

The *Nation* correspondent next interviewed a student to find out what KAU meant to him. "The people are waking up suddenly," the student replied. "They want education so that they can participate in this new world. They don't get it. They don't get jobs of any importance. They can't communicate very well. They are frustrated. So they turn their attention to politics, where they can throw themselves around and seem to be doing something."

The Mau Mau, meanwhile, were getting ready for full-scale guerrilla warfare. Members stole pistols and rifles from white farms, cars and restaurants. So many hundreds of weapons disappeared that the government was forced to threaten a $300 fine and a three-month jail sentence for any whites who lost them.

The full storm of Mau Mau broke out in February, 1952, in the Central Province. The first attacks were sabotage raids against White Highlands farms. Cattle had their legs cut off and crops were set afire. When Queen Elizabeth visited Nairobi briefly that month, five such fires were visible as her plane took off for London.

By September, not a night went by without a glow in the sky over Kikuyuland from a burning farm building, crop or Kikuyu hut whose occupant remained stubbornly Christian.

African politicians on the Legislative Council tried to minimize the Mau Mau threat. "Terrorism? I don't know of any terrorism," insisted the government's chief native commissioner. "There is a small subversive element, to be sure, and there has been a certain amount of trouble, but it has been confined to a small area."

But the burnings and cattle maimings steadily intensified. In the last days of September, fourteen Kikuyu who informed to the police were savagely murdered. At the same time the Forty Group called a secret meeting at Kaloleni Hall in Nairobi to discuss a startling proposal.

The question: whether to assassinate Jomo Kenyatta.

Even though the Mau Mau did not hesitate to use his prestige without permission for their own purposes, they did not trust him. What if the government, frightened by Mau Mau, met Kenyatta's demands and make him part of the power structure in Kenya? There was little doubt that he would suppress Mau Mau and work for peaceful reforms.

But suppose he were to be murdered, and the blame thrown on the government? An infuriated Kenya would rise up behind the Mau Mau in a bloody revolution that would bring them swiftly to power, with all the riches of Kenya theirs alone to plunder. And with no Kenyatta to stop them.

But some felt there was more to be gained by frightening Kenyatta into the ranks of the Mau Mau. So they decided to try this first by giving him an ominous warning he could not mistake—assassinating a close friend of his who worked for the government, Senior Chief Waruhiu. The murder would also serve to frighten other Kikuyu collaborators.

On October 7, 1952, they gunned Waruhiu down in

broad daylight, only seven miles from Nairobi. This bold demonstration of their striking power scared new hundreds of Kikuyu into rushing to the forests to take the Mau Mau oath.

But it failed to intimidate the leader of KAU, who rebuffed hints that he now join forces with the Mau Mau. The Forty Group, meeting after the funeral for Waruhiu, once more discussed plans to murder Jomo Kenyatta.

In mid-October a tough new governor, Sir Evelyn Baring, arrived from England to deal with the crisis. After a quick inspection trip around Kenya, he decided that the country was on the verge of an uprising. He sent an urgent request for the cruiser *Kenya* and a battalion of the Lancashire Fusiliers, who were flown in from the Middle East.

The white settlers were overjoyed that at last the colonial government was going to bare its teeth to the African rebels. They armed themselves for the showdown.

On October 20, 1952, Governor Baring signed a proclamation declaring a state of emergency in Kenya. Announcement of the proclamation was held up for twenty-four hours to give the government an opportunity to make surprise arrests of the six top KAU leaders and get them safely into custody before they could flee to the forests to join Mau Mau forces.

Police broke into Jomo Kenyatta's house at Ichaweri in the predawn hours of October 21, confident of seizing him while he slept. To their chagrin they found him fully dressed, wearing his leather lumber jacket and waiting derisively for their handcuffs. He held his hands out.

"What took you so long, gentlemen?" he scoffed. Obviously warned by the African grapevine, he had chosen to rely on British justice rather than flight.

Neither he nor the police realized that his arrest may have thwarted the decision of the Forty Group to assassinate him.

Bundled off swiftly by truck to an airport, he was flown to detention in a tiny desert outpost in the bleak, arid landscape of Kenya's far north. The government was taking no chance on a mass uprising to liberate him.

It is important to note that at this moment in Kenya's history, with Kenyatta a prisoner, not more than one or two white settlers had been murdered, and Mau Mau oathing ceremonies had not yet entered their most satanic phase. The full horrors of Mau Mau, in other words, began only when Jomo Kenyatta could no longer restrain or direct them—if, indeed, he had ever been able to do either.

Following his arrest, along with five other KAU leaders, almost three hundred other Kikuyu "suspects" were rounded up in the next ten days. Six battalions of the King's Rifles were mustered in Nairobi to reinforce the Lancashire Fusiliers, and armored cars fanned out all over Kikuyuland.

There was no doubt now in any Kikuyu's mind what Governor Baring's "emergency" meant. The white man had declared war—the British government against a tribal society.

The Mau Mau accepted the challenge, forming a Land Freedom Army in the trackless forests. New thousands of Kikuyu flocked to join them voluntarily—even those who had formerly rejected the Mau Mau as evil. They formed guerrilla bands of terrorists determined to kill white men.

What Jomo Kenyatta had struggled all his life to prevent had come to pass. A black and white civil war.

8 ‹‹‹‹‹‹‹‹‹‹‹‹‹‹‹‹‹‹‹

The Trial of Burning Spear

EACH NIGHT THE MAU MAU WOULD MOUNT MIDNIGHT raids, melting back into the forests before dawn. Settlers of the White Highlands protected themselves by having loyal Kipsigis tribesmen, who hated the Kikuyu, stand guard all night in the passageways of their farmhouses. Kipsigis guards were entrusted with rifles, although it now made many of the white settlers unhappy to see guns in *any* black hands.

Striking swiftly, silently and in force, the Mau Mau wiped out whole families of whites, and burned down the villages of loyal natives. "We used to be the meat and the whites were the knives," gloated one Mau Mau leader. "But now *we* are the knives, and the whites are the meat!"

On November 3, 1952, one band of Mau Mau suddenly burst into the farmhouse of white farmer Eric Bowyer, decapitated his houseboys and hacked Bowyer to death. The following month retired Navy Commander E. Meiklejohn and his wife looked up while reading in their Highlands home to see their houseboy leading five Mau Mau into their living room. Both were horribly slashed.

Meiklejohn died, but his wife, left for dead, survived in dreadful condition. Six more Europeans were similarly murdered in this savage fashion before the year ended.

Governor Baring felt only indignation—no guilt.

No white settler dared move around without a gun in his hand or at his belt. Settler wives carried pistols on their hips as they wheeled baby carriages around the yard.

Some settlers enclosed their homes in wire screen to make breaking in more difficult and noisy. Children in the White Highlands were never allowed out of sight of the homestead, and were constantly guarded by Kipsigis. Scrawled Mau Mau notes warned, "You and your family will die—and be sure that your deaths will not be easy!"

Some settlers began to think of leaving Kenya. "It's God's own paradise," one retired army major sighed in a Nairobi cocktail lounge, "but the Devil's own problem!"

Some white settlers began to doubt the wisdom of keeping Jomo Kenyatta under arrest, considering him the one man in Kenya who could stop the Mau Mau outbreak. But the governor turned a deaf ear to any suggestion that he negotiate with the prisoner he accused of "managing" Mau Mau.

To acknowledge Kenyatta's prestige and power would make it impossible to reject his demand for genuine African representation on the Legislative Council any longer. Instead the governor angrily accused him of still being in contact with the Mau Mau while he was being held for trial.

"I do not know what their aims or activities are," Kenyatta denied coolly, "but anything that is harmful to Kenya I denounce." It was a typically inscrutable Kenyatta statement, leaving it up to both Africans and Europeans to interpret as antigovernment or anti-Mau Mau, as they chose.

If any of the prisoners was in secret communication with the Mau Mau, it was more probably Bildad Kaggia, a fierce, bearded Kikuyu fanatic with large hostile eyes who would later rise to eminence and fall again in the shadow of Jomo Kenyatta.

Kenyatta and the other five prisoners were put on trial December 3, 1952. The proceedings lasted five months. As one of the most spectacular trials ever held in a British colony, it commanded worldwide attention. To investigate the deeper meaning of the trial, two British Labor Party MP's, Fenner Brockway and Little Hale, came from London.

"We disagree profoundly with [Colonial Secretary] Oliver Lyttelton," they reported afterward to Parliament, "when he says that social and economic grievances are not the cause of Mau Mau. Mau Mau is an ugly and brutal form of extreme nationalism. It is based on frustration. Frustration brings bitterness, and bitterness brings viciousness."

They strongly opposed the white settlers' demand that KAU be outlawed as a disastrous mistake: "It would intensify bitterness and spread a feeling among Africans that the government is using the crimes of the Mau Mau to strike at legitimate African rights." The way to fight the Mau Mau, they suggested, was to go after the profiteering merchants who had skyrocketed the price of the Africans' staple food, maize flour, by 600 percent since the war.

The Crown deliberately avoided Nairobi for the trial. Instead an obscure little desert town called Kapenguria was chosen as the site. A schoolhouse served as the court. The town had no railroad, a bad road, no telephones and no hotel facilities, and the nearest law library was several days' bumpy travel away in Nairobi. Chief defense counsel Denis N. Pritt, who was brought from England by KAU, protested the "gross, cruel, deliberate injustices worked upon me by the government of Kenya in insisting on having this trial up here."

He had other indignant complaints. Bail had been refused the prisoners, who were kept in the Kapenguria prison. Counsel and witnesses had to sleep in the town of Kitale, thirty miles away. Drinking water had to be hauled to Kapenguria from Kitale, and lawyer Pritt was unable to get a drink of water for the whole first month of the trial. He also charged that his mail was being opened and his phone tapped.

A former judge of the Kenya Supreme Court, Ransley N. Thacker, was called out of retirement to preside over the case. One reporter said wryly, "If he finds Kenyatta guilty, the Mau Mau will murder him. If he doesn't, the white settlers will." The public prosecutor was a lawyer named Somerhough, and the interpreter of Kikuyu was the noted anthropologist Dr. L. S. B. Leakey.

At the outset of the trial, prosecutor Somerhough admitted that although the arrests were made for "managing an unlawful society," he would be unable to establish a direct link between the defendants and Mau Mau terror because the Mau Mau was "a society which has no records." He charged that when the KCA had been declared illegal, it had gone underground as the Mau Mau with Kenyatta as its secret head. KAU was alleged to be Mau Mau's legal, open instrument.

Witnesses called by the prosecution were of dubious character and reliability. Seven years later KAU was able to produce verified evidence that some of them had been bribed to perjure themselves in order to incriminate Kenyatta. When Pritt tried to recall them for cross-examination, Magistrate Thacker hemmed and hawed because of "difficulties."

Kenyatta objected when the government's African witnesses against him were forced to swear oaths only on the Bible. For many natives such oaths had no meaning or binding force, he insisted, and would not make them fear to lie for money. Only true Kikuyu oaths would compel them to tell the truth out of fear of punishment by the god Ngai.

Pritt, an Englishman with great pride in the traditions of the British bar, was deeply upset by the way the cards were being stacked against Kenyatta by the white settlers' version of justice. On December 13 he sent a cable to Labor members of Parliament protesting that a fair trial was impossible under the circumstances.

Judge Thacker, outraged, declared an adjournment while he filed charges against Pritt for contempt of court. The Supreme Court of Kenya, however, threw the charges out. When the trial was reconvened on January 2, 1953, a resentful Judge Thacker manifested no great affection for defense counsel.

In America, the evidence presented by the prosecution in the Kenyatta trial was being widely reported as a prime example of "the world Communist conspiracy" with which Senator Joseph McCarthy was frightening the country before he was condemned by the Senate. In *Life,* Robert Ruark hinted darkly, "I am convinced that Mau Mau's prime exponent, Jomo Kenyatta, now on trial with five of his associates, is by no means his own man. He was educated abroad, boasts of spending several years in Moscow . . . and is highly intelligent."

The bitter court fight went on for five months, played out against an international climate of Western anxiety over communism.

Jomo Kenyatta gave his testimony in English. On the witness stand he told the story of his life as it related to the struggle of Africans against the policies of the colonial government. Asked if KAU believed in violence, he replied, "No, we believe in negotiation." He scored the government's color bar, pointing out, "God did not discriminate when he put the people into the country." Judge Thacker interrupted testily, "These answers are becoming too long; they are tending to become speeches."

During cross-examination Kenyatta handled himself skillfully, adroitly avoiding every trap that sought to link him with terror or the Mau Mau. At the same time he stubbornly refused to denounce any Kikuyu struggling for freedom.

Challenged on his profession of Christianity, he replied that he did not believe in denominations, but insisted that he was "a true Christian believing in God." He admitted practicing polygamy but added, "I do not call it polygamy." Asked if he would swear that he had not stirred up racial enmity against the government, he replied that he would—*unless* the prosecutor considered that to mean "asking for the abolition of the color bar, proper distribution of land, wages for our people, equal representation in Legislative Council."

The prosecution produced a letter seized from his home, the one he had written but not sent to summon KCA leaders to a conference. Did this not prove his connection with the illegal KCA—and therefore with Mau Mau? He calmly explained that he had been mulling over the idea of trying to persuade the KCA leaders to join his legal struggle in KAU.

The prosecutor angrily flourished a newspaper clipping. If Kenyatta had denounced Mau Mau at his rallies, as he claimed to have done, why wasn't the fact reported in the press?

"You will understand," the defendant replied coolly, "that I could not speak for half an hour and be reported accurately in just ten lines." Fifteen more clippings were shown him, many of them longer. Kenyatta shrugged, "I rely more on meetings than the press, because the majority of my audiences cannot read or write."

In rebuttal his own counsel produced a clipping on the Kiambu meeting from the *East African Standard*. This had been the only paper to report the public "curse" on Mau Mau he had pronounced: *"Let Mau Mau disappear, down to the roots of the Mikongoe tree underneath the ground!"* The prosecution conceded that he had said this, but produced a Swahili dictionary to prove that the phrase could have been interpreted as a hint to the Mau Mau to go underground and fight there.

"Absurd," snapped Kenyatta. "It was the equivalent of telling Mau Mau to go and be hanged." When the prosecutor looked scornful, Kenyatta challenged, "If you are doubtful, I ask you to call this forty to fifty thousand people to come here and tell you if they did not understand what I said."

Would he acknowledge, the prosecutor demanded, that it was the English who had abolished slavery in Kenya? Kenyatta admitted that the English "took part" in abolishing slavery, but added caustically that they had substituted land confiscation and forced labor—"so in spite of the fact that slavery was abolished, a new form of slavery was introduced." When he went on in this vein at some length, prosecutor Somerhough interrupted him sarcastically:

"Go on, I am hanging on your lips, go on!"

Kenyatta smiled. "I hope you will not fall."

Laughter swept the courtroom. When the defendant went on to describe the plight of his people under the British, Somerhough assumed a mocking expression.

"If I were to change places with you, sir," Kenyatta said suddenly, "and you become an African, I'll bet you would not endure one week or even two days in that position!"

Once Somerhough appealed in despair to the court to require a "straight" answer out of the witness. Judge Thacker replied, "I think it is interesting. . . ."

The prosecutor looked stunned. "All right," he told Kenyatta weakly, "go on."

Then Thacker concluded dourly, ". . . but I do not want any more of it."

Somerhough beamed.

The prosecutor compelled Kenyatta to admit that, at least from what he had heard, the Mau Mau oath pledged its members to drive the Europeans out of Kenya.

More accusations, based on fragile evidence, came thick and fast. Ever since Kenyatta's return from England in 1946, hadn't he been the secret leader of the illegal KCA? Hadn't he continued to lead it when it emerged as the Mau Mau in 1950? Wasn't he responsible for the "hymn books" that changed the words of such church tunes as "Come Unto Jesus" to "Come Unto Jomo"? Had he not used such hymn books to make Mau Mau a religious cult, with himself its god?

Had he not used KAU as a front organization to recruit Kikuyu into the Mau Mau? Had he not condoned the use of force, terror and extortion in Mau Mau recruiting? Had he not tacitly supported Mau Mau until he himself became alarmed by its growing extremism, and spoken out against it then only to try to restrain it? Weren't all his so-called denunciations of Mau Mau really made with his tongue in cheek, winking at his audience not to take them seriously?

Kenyatta flatly denied every allegation.

"You people have the audacity to ask me silly questions," he finally exploded. "I have done my best, and if all other people had done as I have done, Mau Mau would not be as it is now. *You* made it what it is—not Kenyatta!"

Prosecutor Somerhough looked incredulous. "It is the *government's* fault that Mau Mau exists and goes on?"

"I say *yes!*" Under re-examination by defense counsel he was allowed to elaborate: "The government, instead of joining with us to fight Mau Mau, arrested all the leading members of KAU, accusing them of being Mau Mau. . . . They have arrested thousands of people who would have been useful in helping to put things right in the country. . . . What they wanted to eliminate is the only political organization—KAU—which fights constitutionally for the rights of the African people."

Summing up the case for the defense, Pritt pointed out that the Crown had failed to produce convincing evidence of a link between Kenyatta and the other KAU defendants and Mau Mau. Even if Kenyatta had failed to denounce the terrorist society in his meetings, as the Crown contended, was that a legal basis for convicting him? If so, did the failure of non-African newspapers to report his public curse on Mau Mau constitute legal proof that he had not made it? If so, why had not the Crown permitted the calling of witnesses who had attended that meeting in Kiambu to prove that Kenyatta had, indeed, denounced Mau Mau—and seriously?

As the proceedings wore on, Kenya's gory race war raged in the background, aggravated by reports of the angry clashes between black and white in the courtroom at Kapenguria. On January 1, 1953, two Europeans in the White Highlands were hacked to death as they sat at their dinner table. The following night only the alertness of Kipsigis guards saved two white women from a similar fate.

One week later the Mau Mau abducted two Kikuyu elders of the loyal Gatunda settlement. Terrified of reprisals, no Kikuyu would give information. The government punished the whole clan, reducing it to desperation by confiscating 300 head of cattle and 800 sheep. During January and February other Kikuyu settlements were similarly "fined" a total of 3,000 head of livestock. Proceeds from the sale helped finance the government's costly war against the Mau Mau.

Governor Baring ordered hundreds of thousands of Kikuyu family "squatters" removed from the rich white farms where they served as cheap labor, and had them held on detention reserves. Only those certified "loyal" by screening boards were trucked back for daytime labor. The others were replaced by laborers from other tribes considered "safer."

Many of the exiled squatters had been born on the farms from which they were thrown off. They were not allowed to take with them their cattle, sheep or goats, nor could they harvest any maize they had planted on family plots. Brutality marked the Kikuyu's banishment. Non-Kikuyu laborers would throw small children up on the removal trucks as if they were bundles of firewood. Those uncaught by parents crashed on the floorbeds. Thousands of Kikuyu men, women and children were dragged out of their homes.

Each time the Mau Mau struck, a police dragnet would sweep up hundreds of young male Kikuyu on the nearest reserve for grilling. Soon thousands began fleeing for the forests, preferring the Mau Mau to arrests, accusations, beatings.

The Mau Mau reserved their greatest bitterness for

"traitors"—particularly Kikuyu and Kipsigis who remained loyal to the white man. Far more African informers were killed than Europeans. But now the Mau Mau also added white victims to their lists whenever they could.

On January 24, 1953, they committed a particularly gruesome massacre in the White Highlands by compelling servants of the Roger Ruck family to summon farmer Ruck to a barn on the pretext of "holding an interloper." When Ruck went out to investigate, he was chopped to pieces. His screams brought his wife running with a shotgun. She, too, was massacred. Then the Mau Mau murdered their young son.

On March 26 the Mau Mau climaxed their attacks on the White Highlands with a raid on the loyal Kikuyu settlement of Lari. As night fell a thousand Mau Mau set two hundred Lari huts afire, cutting down men, women and children as they tried to escape. Lari Chief Luka watched each of his eight wives cut to pieces, then was murdered himself.

These Mau Mau atrocities hardly encouraged an unprejudiced, judicial calm in the white man's court at Kapenguria where Jomo Kenyatta's fate was being weighed. As the trial wound to a conclusion and the day of judgment approached, the government took extraordinary precautions throughout Kenya, especially in Nairobi.

Many Africans in Kenya fled to Uganda, fearful that if Kenyatta was acquitted, wrathful white settlers would go on a rampage in a general massacre of all Africans.

But Government House prepared for an opposite reaction.

9 ‹‹‹‹‹‹‹‹‹‹‹‹‹‹‹‹‹‹‹‹‹‹‹

Desert Prisoner

HOPING TO CRUSH THE MAU MAU UPRISING WITH ONE giant hammer blow, the government mounted an attack by a well-trained, well-armed force of 70,000 troops supported by three flights of RAF bombers. Arrayed against them were only 12,000 Land Freedom Army guerrillas armed with knives and a scattering of stolen rifles and pistols.

A cloak of secrecy fell over Crown treatment of captured suspects. Later testimony, however, revealed that white atrocities rivaled the Mau Mau's. Two White Highlanders bound together a pair of suspect Kikuyu by a leather strap around their necks, thrust lighted cigarettes into their ears, flogged them, covered them with paraffin and set them afire.

Another white settler sent Kipsigis forces to raid a Kikuyu village, mistreat the women and burn down the village. A British Army captain ordered multilation of his Kikuyu prisoners with bayonets. Captured Africans were flogged ruthlessly to extract information, many of them dying under the lash. White settlers were allowed to shoot suspect Africans on sight, without fear of being asked embarrassing questions.

There was a lesson to be learned by all nations,

Kenyatta brooded. The more a nation's rulers refused to correct social injustice, the more inevitable they made violent protest. The more violent the protest, the angrier the ruling class would become in outdoing the protesters in harsh retaliation. The upward spiral of violence could only end in either revolution or a brutal police state. Reasoning together was the only intelligent alternative.

But the colonial government refused to yield an inch. Even Christianized Kikuyu were driven into supporting the pagan Mau Mau. Native women sold themselves to government troops for pay in clandestine ammunition for the Land Freedom Army. Kikuyu men who had formerly served the government loyally in army, police and legislative posts began to act as secret agents for the Mau Mau. "Trustworthy" farm workers trucked in from the reserves stole food, ammunition and other supplies for the Mau Mau in the forest.

On the tense morning of April 8, 1953, to a melodramatic crash of thunder and flash of lightning, Judge Thacker delivered his verdict. All of the accused KAU defendants were found guilty of all charges except those blaming them for the controversial sacrilegious hymn books. The magistrate condemned Kenyatta in particular for having let loose "a flood of misery and unhappiness affecting the lives of all the races . . . including your own people."

Kenyatta was stunned but hardly surprised, since he had not allowed himself to expect justice from a colonial court. When he rose to make his final statement, he knew that he was no longer speaking to the colonial government, but over their heads to the courts of English and world opinion.

"On behalf of my colleagues I wish to say that we are not guilty," he declared firmly, "and we do not accept your findings. . . . This case, from our point of view, has been so arranged as to make scapegoats of us in order to strangle the Kenya African Union. . . . We look forward to the day when peace shall come to this land and that the truth shall be known that we, as African leaders, have stood for peace."

He concluded, "None of us would be happy or would condone the mutilation of human beings. We are humans and we have families. . . . We stand for the rights of the African people that Africans may find a place among the nations."

"You have much to answer for," replied a grim-faced Judge Thacker, "and for that you will be punished. The maximum sentences which this court is empowered to pass are the sentences which I do pass, and I can only comment that in my opinion they are inadequate for what you have done."

He sentenced each of the defendants to seven years' imprisonment at hard labor, and also recommended to the government that Kenyatta be held in restriction for the rest of his natural life in the remote Northern Province.

The celebrated prisoner was handcuffed and swiftly flown north to tiny Lokitaung, a harsh desert wasteland on the Sudan-Ethiopian border. His first glimpse of this dreary outpost revealed a lunar landscape of lava rubble and rock ruled by a blistering sun and dust storms.

My home, he reflected soberly, *for the rest of my life.* With aching nostalgia he thought of the beautiful pastures bending softly under the cool breezes of the White Highlands. Then he shook off the tormenting images as self-pity.

It was quickly made clear to him that while he might be a demigod to the Kikuyu and a folk hero to the rest of Kenya, in Lokitaung he would be subject to the same indignities and hardships as ordinary Crown prisoners. He shrugged, amused that his captors didn't realize that the more they martyred him, the more sympathizers his cause would win.

He was forced to enter camp by wading through an eye-stinging cattle dip, beaten over the head by warders' clubs until he submerged completely. The camp itself was a prison compound surrounded by high rolls of barbed wire. Crude stone blockhouses with corrugated iron roofs held thirteen prisoners apiece, bedded on the concrete floor.

"In prison I was just a mere convict, known by number, not by name," Kenyatta recalled later. "I was told that was one of the punishments, to deny me all the privileges that I had before. I was treated just like a common prisoner."

He stood out like a giant among the other prisoners, however, this powerful figure with a great grizzled, bearded head. His cool, deep voice, fatherly and benevolent one moment, could thunder harshly the next. His moods were unpredictable. Sometimes he was enigmatic or droll, his eyes mischievous. Other times, when he was bitter, they flashed with fire.

From the moment of his arrival the other prisoners unanimously recognized him as camp leader. His blockhouse inmates elected him their cook, the most popular prison job. Once a week he called committee meetings of representatives from each blockhouse to discuss prison problems. He also held classes after work to educate illiterate prisoners and teach them Kenya's history of pre-European days.

He kept his own mind sharp by reading and rereading every book he could get his hands on. "I have read practically all the principal religions," he later declared. "I read them all in prison." Asked which of the religious faiths he respected most, he replied, "I'm a Christian. I believe in the teachings of Christ, which many so-called Christians do not follow. I've no quarrel with them— they can do what they like. But I believe in Christianity as Jesus taught it." That, he felt, precluded belonging to any sects.

His favorite pastime was playing checkers with prisoners whose jobs around officers' houses let them peek at a newspaper or overhear radio broadcasts. Their whispered reports kept him in touch with political developments.

On June 8, 1953, he learned that the government had banned KAU and arrested its vice-president, Luo leader F. W. Odede. He shook his head incredulously. When would the white settlers ever learn? Now many Luo would join the Kikuyu in the only avenue of protest left open—Mau Mau.

Even one of the moderate African politicians admitted to the Legislative Council felt compelled to protest.

"African mistrust of the white man is now widespread," sighed Dr. Gikonyo Wa Kiano. "The discrepancy between the white man's professed democracy and religion and his behavior toward Africans has become so glaringly evident that practically anything proposed by any white man is, *a priori,* subject to suspicion and mistrust."

Meanwhile, an appeal of the verdict against Kenyatta was pressed by barrister Pritt in the Kenya Supreme Court. The prisoner waited skeptically for British justice as practiced in England to manifest itself in Kenya.

"Whatever the court decides," observed *The New York Times,* "the established order finds itself in an almost impossible predicament. . . . Independent of what happens in the courtroom it is the jailed Kenyatta and his doctrine of the essential superiority of the African way of life that is gaining in stature through the publicity."

Pritt argued the appeal with the aid of A. P. Kapila, a Hindu lawyer from Nairobi, suggesting to many that defense funds were coming largely from the East Indian population seeking to end the white-controlled caste system of Kenya.

Thrilling news reached Kenyatta over the checkerboard. The Kenya Supreme Court ruled that Magistrate Thacker had had no jurisdiction in the Rift Valley Province where the trial had been held, making it illegal. Kenyatta and the other five KAU defendants were remanded for a new trial before the East African Appeals Court.

Prisoners in Lokitaung faced Mount Kenya, palms upraised as they chanted in prayer: "Oh, Ngai, help our leader Kenyatta, and help all the other leaders of the Africans, who are striving to free us from the chains of slavery, in the East and the West, from the North to the South."

Similar prayers, Kenyatta learned, were being said for him in prison camps all over Kenya, on the crowded reserves and in the city slums.

But on August 22 black nationalist hopes were dashed when the Appeals Court upheld the prison term. Pritt immediately appealed the decision to the Privy Council in London, highest court in the British Commonwealth.

A realist, Kenyatta now steeled himself to the grim prospect of remaining a political prisoner for the rest of his life—or until some miraculous event turned all the faces of the Legislative Council in Nairobi black.

The Appeals Court decision seemed to touch off a fresh wave of brutality toward Kenyatta and other political prisoners. For failing to address a European respectfully as *Effendi,* they would be imprisoned for a day in earth dungeons—holes in the ground roofed by steel that became broilers under the equatorial sun. Sadistic guards would sell them forbidden tobacco, then tip off other guards who would search and find it, dragging them off for punishment.

When their frustrations grew too great to bear, Kenyatta and his fellow prisoners would brawl in the blistering heat until exhausted, then sink into a state of hopeless apathy and despair. Once Kenyatta was caught drinking some *mukoma* (fermented beer) smuggled in to ease his misery.

He was thrown into a corrugated iron cell, six by four feet, without food or water for five days. By the fifth day he lay gasping for breath on the concrete floor, sick and delirious. Barely alive when they released him on the fifth day, he wearily wished they had let him die.

When his leg became badly infected, he was shipped to Lodwar prison hospital seventy-five miles south. Prayers for his recovery rose from every hut in the compound. Tears of sentiment trickled through his whitened beard as he heard them.

At Lodwar he was freshly embittered by news of atrocities against his people in government "screening camps." Torture was being used against Kikuyu women as well as men "detainees" to make them confess to Mau Mau membership. European officers were discreetly absent when non-Kikuyu African guards used torture, but Kenyatta knew that the guards would never have dared to use these tactics without orders.

Detainees were also forced to chant in chorus: "Englishmen will rule this country forever. Jomo Kenyatta is a dog. Mau Mau is bad." Many muttered instead, in Kikuyu, "Englishmen will *not* rule this country forever.

Jomo Kenyatta is a god. Mau Mau is grand." Their defiance persisted even when guards who understood beat them mercilessly.

The more the colonial government sought to repress Mau Mau by brutal methods, the more brutal Mau Mau reprisals became. Grass-roots support for the rebels grew steadily all over Kenya as they won recognition as a Land Freedom Army. A "passive wing" of sympathizers helped supply the fighters in the forests. At least 90 percent of the Kikuyu, and a good proportion of other tribes, now supported Mau Mau.

The government might control the legal courts, but the Mau Mau had its underground courts. These passed death sentences on Africans who collaborated with the European enemy. Against white power—armies, money, authority and control—the Africans posed black power —terror, guerrilla warfare, nationalist pride and a hunger for their lost lands.

Many of the insurrectionists were fanatics dedicated to the cause of Africa for the Africans—willing to fight and even kill their own people for food and guns, to bring about a black Kenya guided by Jomo Kenyatta.

For four incredible years they were able to defy the colonial government and the imperial might of Great Britain behind it. They made guns out of bicycle frames, pipes and door bolts. Bottles filled with stolen explosives became bombs. But their real secret weapon was popular support.

By day Kikuyu women obediently built defense palisades of sharpened bamboo stakes, as directed by government forces, to keep Mau Mau out of the reserves. But by night they stole out to the forests with food and supplies for the Land Freedom Army. Some soldiers in the King's African Rifles were not above passing along arms to civilians working at their barracks. When Africans in the Government Home Guard were sent out on patrol, many looked the wrong way.

Kenyatta was saddened by the senseless tragedy of the conflict. Had the government left him free, and had it negotiated grievances with KAU, Britain could have remained in Kenya as a benevolent trustee of African self-determination. Instead it had chosen to crush protest, and now all were reaping the bloody harvest of autocratic stubbornness.

The British sought to bomb the forest fighters into submission. But crashing explosives in the densely wooded Aberdare Mountains around Mount Kenya failed to find their targets. The Mau Mau simply lit fake campfires for the British to waste bombs on, laughing as they slipped safely back into other parts of the forest.

In April, 1954, the chagrined British tried a new maneuver called Operation Anvil. They sought to cut Mau Mau supply lines by using African trackers to hem the forest fighters in and draw a tight cordon around their positions. White Kenyan police with blackened faces combed the mountains for guerrilla hideouts. Steadily narrowing "prohibited areas," they shot any Africans within them on sight. Broader trails were cut into the heart of the forests.

This tightening noose choked off the Land Freedom Army's communication lines with its secret headquarters in the Nairobi slums. By May, 1954, the British had killed or wounded over 5,000 Mau Mau "suspects" and arrested almost 160,000 Kikuyu. In another year they ground down the fighting strength of the Land Freedom Army to a hard-core force of 5,000 men.

This last-ditch force was penned off from the White Highlands by a huge fifty-mile ditch filled with stakes and barbed wire. Then Kikuyu women who had lost husbands and sons to Mau Mau terrorists were sent into the forest with long bush knives to flush out pockets of hiding guerrillas.

Military victory seemed to stiffen British intransigence. Word reached Kenyatta that the Privy Council in London had rejected his appeal. A jubilant Governor Baring ordered his land at Ichaweri confiscated, and his home was burned down to prevent its being turned into a Kikuyu shrine.

Even after Kenyatta had finished his prison sentence, Baring reassured anxious white settlers and tribesmen loyal to the Crown, he would still be held in restriction in the north and refused permission to return to Kikuyuland.

Deeply depressed by all these setbacks, Kenyatta began to develop morbid fears that the colonial government intended to poison him. Feeling now that his cause was utterly lost, and he along with it, he began drinking heavily. Some suspected that the strong native brew was smuggled in to him with tacit government approval, in the hope that alcoholism would destroy his prestige and influence among Africans.

Yet even in the hours of his own despair, the cause of freedom and justice for black Kenya for which he had fought so tirelessly persevered. Growing pressure came from all over the world for his release and an end to colonialism in Kenya. The British Labor Party accused the Conservative government of having betrayed the ideals of British justice.

The chagrined colonial government of Kenya itself was coming to realize that the African volcano of nationalism, having burst its cone open, was going to remain in a constant state of eruption. Slowly, reluctantly, it began to make concessions. More Africans were put on the Legislative Council. Most of the 80,000 Kikuyu held behind barbed wire were released, with a promise to investigate police brutality. Committees were set up to study the use of natives as underpaid slave labor and the confiscation of Kikuyu land.

But Kenyatta knew that the white settlers were too late with too little. The hour of accommodation had passed.

The price for peace was now *Uhuru*—black freedom!

10 ←←←←←←←←←←←←←←←←←←

"Uhuru Kenyatta! Uhuru Kenya!"

SOME EUROPEANS, ASHAMED OF WHAT KENYA'S COLONIAL government had done, sought racial reconciliation by making private gestures of compassion. One English-woman visited a detention compound with her baby, which she let be held and passed around a circle of Kikuyu women anyone of whom might have been bit ter enough to dash the white infant to the ground. In-stead they clucked over the baby like mothers anywhere in the world, then gently handed him back to the coura-geous white mother.

But the new conciliatory tone of the white power structure, Kenyatta knew, was based not on compassion but fear, fear not only of the Mau Mau and persistent revolutionary sabotage, but also of a newer threat—African labor unions.

In April, 1955, a dock strike broke out at Mombasa —the first organized strike in Kenya's history. It was led by Oxford-educated Tom Mboya, a Luo who had risen rapidly to African leadership in the absence of Kenyatta. The white settlers demanded that Governor Baring force 10,000 Kikuyu detainees to serve as strike-breakers. Hearing of this plan, outraged Labor Party members in

115

the English Parliament spiked it as a violation of the rules of the Geneva Convention.

Mboya's strike was victorious. The dockworkers won an unprecedented salary raise of 33 percent. Delighted by news of this first African labor victory, Kenyatta determined that if he were ever released, Tom Mboya would be one of the bright young Africans he would want at his right hand.

By the end of 1956, British military operations against the Land Freedom Army were in the mopping-up stage. The statistics of victory were appalling. Government troops had killed over 11,000 in warfare; hung 1,000 as criminals; captured almost 3,000; and rounded up 80,000 Kikuyu suspected of being Mau Mau supporters in concentration camps.

In contrast, their own losses had been incredibly light—only 32 white civilians, 57 members of the security forces and 1,740 African loyalists killed by terrorists.

All this, Kenyatta reflected bitterly, because the government preferred to believe that he was behind Mau Mau. Ironically, the government had actually gone broke by pushing Kenya into a state of civil war. From a surplus of several million dollars in the treasury before declaring the emergency, it had plunged heavily into debt, even with London reluctantly paying half the cost of Operation Anvil. The Mau Mau hunt, the detention camps and extra police had cost $200 million.

And in the end the Africans had lost their war but won their cause. Freedom for African nations was "blowing in the wind." By 1957 Libya, Eritrea, Morocco, Tunisia and Ghana had already become independent. The days of colonialism in Africa were obviously numbered.

The apprehensive white farmers of Kenya began looking around for buyers, especially after union-backed pressure from Tom Mboya forced the government to let Africans vote in a May, 1957, national election. The "whispering vote" was enormous. Illiterate Africans who had never held a pencil and didn't know how to mark a ballot had their votes cast for them by whispering their choices to presumably honest polling station officials.

These primitive elections raised African membership on the Legislative Council from four appointees to fourteen elected representatives, while European membership went from eleven to fourteen. This was progress, but still far from democratic representation, since less than 50,000 white settlers now had an equal voice with 5,500,000 Africans. The colonial government counted on tribal rivalries to prevent a bloc black vote, knowing that white representatives would vote as a unit.

To keep the African vote divided, the government barred the largest and strongest tribe in Kenya from participating in the election. Only the Kikuyu could have forged a solid coalition of Africans in the Legislative Council.

The Luo were not fooled. Tom Mboya promptly demanded another fifteen African seats on the Council. Calling for all emergency decrees to be rescinded, thus restoring Kikuyu rights, he insisted that the government recognize the inevitability of African self-government.

"Your time is past," he told Europeans in a speech before a cheering crowd of Africans. "Get out of Africa!" He insisted upon the immediate release of Jomo Kenyatta to head a new, free African government of Kenya.

Fresh hope buoyed the famous prisoner as he followed the rapid developments of the independence movement and the crusade to free him. To prepare himself for the rigors of a return to active political life, he abruptly stopped drinking and even gave up smoking.

117

Further inspiration came in news that Ghana, under his old friend Kwame Nkrumah, had won independence. He, too, had a rendezvous with destiny.

A new, influential champion took up his cause—Jaromogi "Oginga" Odinga, a Luo elected to the Legislative Council from Central Nyanza. Along with Tom Mboya, Odinga demanded Kenyatta's immediate release as the leader of all black Kenya.

On all sides the cry rose in deafening clamor:

"Uhuru na Kenyatta!"

In April, 1959, the desperate government finally released him from Lokitaung. But he was still held in indefinite restriction in the almost equally remote village of Lodwar, where he once had been hospitalized. Asked later about Lodwar, Kenyatta described it wryly as "freedom and dust." There was more liberty for him at Lodwar, but seasonal dust storms blotted out everything and everyone.

To appease the public outcry, he was given a small cottage and even an allowance with which to buy government-approved newspapers and books. His spirits perked further at the end of the year when the government finally declared the seven-year-old Mau Mau emergency to be at an end.

Significantly, for the first time in Kenya's history a white man was sentenced to death for murdering an African, despite furious protests from the white settlers.

But despite these evidences of change of heart, the colonial government still dreaded the release of Kenyatta as signifying the end of British rule in Kenya. To justify keeping him in detention, it released the Corfield Report, a one-sided White Paper. Using selected trial testimony, it insisted that Kenyatta "did his utmost to conceal the savage and revolutionary Mau Mau movement behind a facade of . . . nationalism." Ian Macleod, Colonial Secretary in Britain's Conservative Cabinet, agreed.

KAU leaders continued to deny hotly that their organization had had anything to do with the Mau Mau outbreak. KAU's real crime in the eyes of the colonial government, they charged, was simply their struggle against colonialism.

"I was doing all I could to avoid violence," Kenyatta replied to the Corfield Report, "and in many cases I denounced violence in my political meetings. My denunciations were not given wide publicity because for one reason or another the government wanted to paint me as black as they could. They tried to put all the evil things on me."

In the fall of 1960 the Colonial Secretary agreed to hold a conference of native and white leaders of Kenya at Lancaster House in London, to rearrange the Legislature and Legislative Council for fairer African representation.

To placate Kenya's Africans, the Lancaster Conference drew up a new constitution reserving only ten seats in the Legislature for Europeans, while opening thirty-three to free election. Africans were given four seats on the Legislative Council to every three for the Europeans. In exchange, Thurgood Marshall of the United States was asked to draft a Bill of Rights for minorities (Europeans and Asians) which African politicians who came to power would be pledged to respect.

Tom Mboya and James Gichuru made direct representations to the Colonial Secretary for the release of Jomo Kenyatta.

"We do not believe his release will reverse Kenya into violence," Mboya declared. "We refuse to believe that he is inherently an evil man." Kenyatta was not freed, but the ban against KAU was lifted; Gichuru,

Mboya and Odinga reorganized it as the Kenya African National Union (KANU), to emphasize that it represented a tribal coalition.

When the African delegation returned from London, Gichuru addressed a KANU meeting on November 13, 1960.

"We are no longer begging for *Uhuru* from the Europeans and Asians," he told a wildly cheering crowd. "They will soon have to kneel before *us!*"

As the new elections approached, the worried colonial government sought votes for white candidates by announcing a land resettlement program, opening up the restricted White Highlands to Africans. Indignant white settlers appealed this edict to London. When the Colonial Secretary rejected their appeal, many began to feel that there was no longer any future for the white man in Kenya. They began to hold back new investments and ship liquid capital abroad.

In eight months of 1960 over $30 million was drained from Kenya's economy, causing a severe business slump. Many whites and Asians began planning to leave the country.

To make matters worse, the government badly bungled the land resettlement program. The wrong Kikuyu families received the available open land in the White Highlands. None of the 20,000 Kikuyu on the reserves who received land were families who formerly had homes there.

Far from being conciliated by the government's clumsy act of contrition, nearly half of Kenya's African population—Kikuyu, Luo and Kamba—united together in KANU to press for independence. Gichuru, Mboya and Odinga made it clear to the government that they considered their real leader to be Kenyatta by electing the Crown's famous prisoner to the Presidency of KANU *in absentia.*

This act of defiance angered the new governor, Sir Patrick Renison. It had made KANU illegal, he announced coldly, and therefore he could not register KANU as a legal party with the right to run candidates in the new election.

The three KANU leaders decided that discretion at this point might be wiser than confrontation. So Gichuru became Acting President, sending private assurances to Jomo Kenyatta that he would step down for *Mzee* as soon as KANU could win his freedom. Odinga became Vice-President, with Mboya as Secretary. Their persistent demand for Kenyatta's release served notice on Governor Renison that this would be made a major political issue in KANU's election campaign.

He replied stiffly that he would not free the African leader, whom he accused of having led his people into "darkness and death." Renison made it clear, furthermore, that he was not fond of KANU because of its largely Kikuyu and Luo coloration. The government intended to do everything it could to help a new opposition African party.

The Kenya African Democratic Union (KADU) was a largely government-inspired coalition of minority tribes—Masai, Baluhya, Nandi, Kipsigis and others who feared the land-hungry Kikuyu. Government strategy was to split the African vote between KANU and KADU, so that the white power structure could continue to rule Kenya by manipulating KADU.

As Kenyatta anxiously followed developments from Lodwar, it became clear that KANU was not going to have an easy time gaining the necessary political power to win his freedom. KANU began the election campaign

121

of November, 1960, by planning a big meeting in the Masai reserve to win the Masai away from KADU. But the unsophisticated Masai were alarmed by truckloads of Kikuyu rolling into their reserve to attend the meeting. Fearing a tribal invasion, Masai warriors attacked the trucks, spearing one Kikuyu.

Dissension was rife within the ranks of KANU itself. Odinga and Mboya heartily disliked and distrusted each other. Odinga led a factional attack on both Mboya and Gichuru, spreading rumors that they were insincere in demanding Kenyatta's release, having privately assured the government they did not really oppose his detention. Mboya indignantly denounced the rumor as a lie. At a dramatic mass meeting in Nairobi, he and Gichuru publicly signed a pledge of loyalty to Jomo Kenyatta.

Almost all African candidates for office swore their loyalty to *Mzee* in their political oratory. Campaign meetings were held all over the country, ranging from rural gatherings under the trees to crowds of 20,000 at Fort Hall. The governor now permitted once-forbidden tribal dances and rites as part of the meetings, making them gay occasions.

Kenya seethed with excitement on February 28, 1961, as the nation's masses flocked to the polling stations for what everyone recognized to be the first fully democratic national election. In Nairobi elegantly dressed wives of white settlers cast their votes knowing that now they were outnumbered at the polls by Turkana tribeswomen of the far northwest, dressed in skins and claw necklaces, who lined up holding voting registration cards in cleft sticks.

White candidates, many of whom had prudently campaigned with "safe" Africans on a coalition ticket, waited anxiously for the first returns to reveal whether their strategy had worked. In dust-choked Lodwar, Kenyatta, too, waited tensely for the results that would determine his fate.

The final tally showed that KANU, with 467,000 votes, had won a sweeping victory over KADU, with only 142,000. KANU now had eighteen seats in the new Legislative Council, while KADU had only eleven. KANU was now the majority party of Kenya and as such entitled to form the new government. But KANU's leaders flatly refused to do so until Governor Renison freed Kenyatta to head it.

Renison rejected their demand. If Kenyatta was released, he knew, the party would close ranks solidly behind him, and it would be the beginning of the end of the British in Kenya. On the other hand, if Renison could buy time by compelling KANU to form a government without Kenyatta, a power struggle between Odinga and Mboya could split and destroy their party. Renison could then offer the more moderate Mboya the leadership of a coalition government with KADU leaders.

But Renison's refusal to free Kenyatta even after the election sent a shock wave of anger through the country. To all Africans *Mzee* was by now not only the true leader of all tribes, but also the very symbol of Kenyan nationalism and independence. Unrest boiled up swiftly. Mau Mau just released from detention began reswearing secret oaths.

Paul Ngei, one of the five who had been sentenced with Kenyatta, called a huge protest meeting. "Africans were made beggars in their own country while Europeans farmed comfortably on the Highlands," he shouted. "These Europeans must have their farms taken from them! This is *our* country!"

Alarmed white moderates in the Legislature put pressure on Renison to free Kenyatta before a new and more terrible wave of Mau Mau plunged Kenya into another bloodbath.

"We're only making him a legendary god by keeping him shielded from responsibility," one legislator pleaded with the governor. "Bring him out of the clouds of Mount Kenya into the government. Let him make a mess of trying to run the country without white cooperation. That's the only way we can end the myth of Kenyatta the great leader!"

But Renison moved cautiously. For one thing, Kenyatta had flatly refused to make any statement revealing his plans for the government. For another, letting him go free would make him a greater hero than ever, touching off a great surge of African emotion. Release of the supratribal "father figure" would be taken as a certain sign that the colonial government, by caving in to KANU pressure, was weak.

So on March 1 Renison made a national radio broadcast which he hoped would avert disaster and permit him to save face and gain time. He repeated that Mr. Kenyatta would not be released until after a new African government had been formed and found workable. In a few weeks, however, Mr. Kenyatta would be moved from Lodwar to Maralal. As soon as the new government was formed, its ministers, along with religious leaders and journalists, would be allowed to visit Maralal and consult with Mr. Kenyatta.

Maralal was a pleasant mountain oasis at the northern edge of the Rift Valley, much more accessible from Nairobi. But perhaps the most significant indication of how much times had changed was that the same African politician whom Renison had called "a leader to darkness and death," referring to him as plain Jomo Kenyatta, was now suddenly dignified with the respectful prefix of "Mister."

In that one word the colonial government grudgingly conceded that Kenyatta was not the savage criminal they had made him out to be in order to jail him, but an African patriot fighting for his country's independence.

Despite these concessions, it became clear that no operative or valid government could even be formed without the approval of Kenyatta. So on March 23, 1961, a delegation of combined KANU and KADU leaders, including Gichuru, Odinga and Mboya for KANU, were permitted to visit him in Maralal. They brought him word that the government had agreed to build a new house for him and his family in his home district of Kiambu, to replace the one destroyed to prevent its becoming an African shrine. It would be ready for Mr. Kenyatta, Renison promised, upon his release, "in due course."

Kenyatta's wife and daughters, meanwhile, were being allowed to join him in Maralal. But Kenyatta, after so many years of political persecution, was not to be bought off cheaply. He approved two KANU decisions—to refuse participation in any government until his unconditional release, and to demand independence for Kenya by the end of the year.

Excited foreign correspondents jammed into Government House to learn from Sir Renison what Kenyatta intended doing about the chaotic political situation in Kenya.

"Gentlemen," sighed the governor in frustration, "*I* don't know what is on Mr. Kenyatta's mind!"

11 ‹‹‹‹‹‹‹‹‹‹‹‹‹‹‹‹‹‹‹‹‹‹‹

A Man Is Freed

PERHAPS IN THE HOPE OF SOLVING THE ENIGMA HIMSELF, Renison allowed sixty journalists to fly north to Maralal, permitting Kenyatta to hold his first press conference since his arrest nine years earlier. *Mzee* received them with a small ironic smile. Only yesterday he had been beaten and whipped as a common criminal. Now suddenly reporters from all over the world were hanging on every word he uttered.

Answering questions for three hours, he told them that he had always advocated nonviolence, and planned to achieve freedom for Kenya by constitutional means. In the new Kenya he foresaw, all would be treated equally—Africans, Europeans and Asians—with no special privileges for anyone. He denied all Communist ties, insisting there was no place for communism in African society. The Corfield Report?

"A pack of lies," he said simply.

He credited the new constitution worked out in the London Conference for having brought about honest elections. But now that Africans had won a majority in the Legislature, the colonial government must step down and allow them to take the remaining steps toward full self-government.

"This is the real basis of the government's reluctance to release him, for all the talk about his being 'a security risk,' " the London *Times* correspondent cabled to his paper. "The fear is that his release would lead to sustained pressure for more and more concessions until total independence had been attained."

One week later Ronald Ngala, leader of the KADU opposition party, agreed to form a new government with support from white members of the Legislative Council. KANU's leaders expressed their contempt for any African party that would let itself be used as a front for the white power structure.

"We are not going *into* government," Ngala pleaded. "We *are* the government. We are not just cooperating with a colonial administration." But he knew that without Kenyatta's release and KANU's participation, a KADU government would quickly be discredited and repudiated.

Meanwhile at Maralal the stream of visitors to the house of the famous prisoner was endless. He would welcome them in the doorway with a warm bear hug. They came like reverent pilgrims to Mecca, seeing in *Mzee* the one great African leader able to rise above all tribal and personal rivalries, unite the country and lead it to independence. For most Africans he was the living spirit of Kenya itself.

His warmest embraces were reserved for released political prisoners. He felt a strong kinship with other Africans who had felt the stinging whip of the guard, roasted in the merciless tropic sun, writhed in the punishment pits. One of them brought an exciting rumor— the Government was about to order his release. Kenyatta was skeptical.

But it was true. To Governor Renison's chagrin, Ronald Ngala had found it impossible to function as

Prime Minister in the face of African indignation. "I will be unable to stay in office," he told the governor flatly, "unless Kenyatta is freed immediately." Renison was cornered. Having thwarted KANU, he saw KADU as his only alternative.

On August 15, 1961, the great day for which the seventy-one-year-old "Burning Spear" of Kenya had long been waiting came at last. A police plane was flown to Maralal to bring him, his wife Ngina and their four daughters home from exile.

He felt dazed, almost incredulous, as the little plane left behind the bleak northland where he had spent the last nine grim years. It seemed like a dream to be outside the compound barbed wire, free at last from the control of brutal guards. Strangely, he felt drained of the bitterness that had once raged within him like lava. He felt only a glow of love for his people, who had not forgotten him, and whose loyalty had finally forced open the doors of his prison.

He was deeply stirred by a welcome-home rally in Nairobi to which over 30,000 Africans flocked in joyful delirium. Not only Kikuyu but thousands from other tribes were among his eager venerators. Barefoot women danced without restraint to an exciting thunder of drums, shrilling enthusiastically, "Kenyatta is home! Thank you, Jomo!"

All of Kenya seemed to shake in the tremendous ovation that greeted the first glimpse of the huge, powerful figure, clad in black leather jacket and tribal cap, as he mounted the speaking platform. Acknowledging the acclaim by waving a zebra-tail fly whisk, he called out happily, *"Uhuru!"*

A KANU spokesman introduced him to the enormous crowd as "a second god, Jomo Kenyatta!" Waiting for the deafening tumult to subside, he held aloft his ornamented fly whisk like a royal scepter. When he could finally be heard, his deep, authoritative voice thrilled all who remembered it.

Hanging on to his every word, they were overjoyed that he had lost none of his old power to stir them to tears or rage, as well as discharge their frustrations with a mockery of the white establishment that moved them to laughter. His piercing eyes, moving hypnotically back and forth over his audience, held them enthralled.

He did not dwell on their past struggles, nor rehearse the injustices he had suffered at the hands of the colonial government. He threatened no enemy or rival with reprisals. Such backward-looking bitterness, Kenyatta now felt, would be suitable for a tribal chieftain, but not for an African national leader who would have to unite all factions, black and white, in a great struggle to forge a new Kenya.

"It is the future, my friends, that is living, and the past that is dead," he told his followers. "In all that I have seen, in many countries and at many periods of my life, never has there seemed any purpose in arguments about the past, or any nobility in motives of revenge."

He called for a Kenya without prejudice, where citizens of all races and colors would be treated as equals, working together in harmony. The slogan for Kenya, he urged, was no longer just *Uhuru* but *Uhuru na Moja* (Freedom and Unity).

It was the speech of a revolutionist whom time and suffering had matured to the stature of a statesman.

He toured the country speaking to millions of Kenyans who clamored to see him in person. A whole new generation had come of age without ever having beheld him, knowing him only as the legendary symbol of the emerging new nation.

But wherever he went he was instantly recognized by his towering figure, beard, silver-handled fly whisk and blackwood cane. Crowds were magnetized, crying out, *"Baba Wa Taifa"* (Father of the Nation).

One enthusiastic devotee told a crowd earnestly, "Mr. Kenyatta was chosen by God to lead Kenya, just as Moses was chosen to take the Israelites out of Egypt!"

Kenyatta's greatest acclaim came, as always, from the adoring women of his country. Bringing him endless gifts of goats, pigs, sheep, cows and baskets of corn, they shrilled with delight when he told crowds gravely, "Of course, the world cannot exist without ladies—an important species!"

The more black Kenya hailed him as a deliverer, the more white Kenya watched him with bitter suspicion. To the European settlers of the Highlands, he was a cynical, cunning, bloodthirsty criminal and political adventurer. The foreign press suspected that the real Kenyatta was probably a shrewd, ambitious African politician who was personally dedicated to freedom and equality for Africans.

Whatever the truth about him, it was clear that he now held all the winning cards and that time was rapidly running out for colonialism in this region of Africa.

In October, 1961, James Gichuru kept his promise and stepped down as president of KANU, just as he had turned over the presidency of KAU upon Kenyatta's return to Kenya after the war. As the new head of KANU, Kenyatta became the open leader of the opposition, but majority, party.

His second step up the ladder of power came three months later when a KANU member of the Legislative Council resigned in his favor. Governor Renison quickly huddled with Prime Minister Ngala to strengthen

131

KADU by a decentralization plan that divided Kenya into seven autonomous regions. Renison hoped that tribal regionalism would keep the country too fractured to unite behind Kenyatta for independence. Ngala was also allowed to announce a plan to transfer one million European acres to landless Africans and to promote more Africans to better jobs.

In April, 1962, Renison sought to sidetrack Kenyatta by appointing him Minister of State for Constitutional Affairs and Economic Planning, hoping this sinecure would pacify him and keep him too busy to demand total power.

As he entered the councils of power, from which he had been barred all his life, Kenyatta seemed a little stunned and bewildered at first. The climb from prisoner to cabinet minister had been swift and dizzying.

The press and KANU cynics observed that he seemed muddled and indecisive, apparently confused by the abrupt change from challenging power to wielding it. He also seemed helpless to control the clashes within KANU between the Communist-oriented faction of Odinga and the West-leaning Mboya group.

The white settlers rejoiced that the great "witch doctor of independence" they had dreaded was turning out to be just another empty, overmagnified Wizard of Oz.

Gradually, however, Kenyatta adjusted to being part of the establishment instead of outside it. He seemed to shake off the effects of nine years' imprisonment like a tough old boxer recovering from a knockdown. Regaining his old vigor and dynamism, he forced Mboya and Odinga to end their disruptive feuding for his mantle by making it clear that *he* intended to be wearing it for a long time to come.

He led KANU in a vigorous, unified campaign in

the 1963 parliamentary elections. On May 27 KANU scored a sweeping victory over KADU, winning 64 out of 112 seats in the new House of Representatives, plus the support of six independent candidates. Kenyatta's party also won 19 of 38 Senate seats, with the support of two independents. The only white candidate who had ventured to run in the elections was beaten so badly he had to forfeit his filing fee.

On June 1 the former British prisoner, whom the London *Times* had once predicted would spend the rest of his life behind barbed wire, became the new Prime Minister of the Crown colony and protectorate. The glum colonial government handed over to him the key posts of Defense, External Affairs and Internal Security. British rule was now only a technicality. Real power in Kenya belonged to Kenyatta.

The whole nation awaited his first cabinet appointments with intense interest as an indication of the wave of the future. Europeans would breathe easier if he favored Mboya over Odinga, forecasting a capitalist-style development of Kenya with strong Western ties.

Kenyatta respected Mboya's grasp of world affairs and brilliance as a parliamentarian. But he also distrusted the young politician as an arrogant, ruthless demagogue of dubious loyalty and a quick-witted opportunist.

On the other hand, Oginga Odinga—"Double-O" as his friends called him—was important to Kenyatta as chief of the Luo, with strong support among civil servants and urban youth. An erratic, emotional radical who freely admitted taking money from both Moscow and Peking, Odinga nevertheless denied that he was a Communist or under any obligation to any Communist power. Kenyatta saw him as a shrewd opportunist who appreciated the value of a left-wing posture and connections. As a onetime recipient himself of Communist largesse, Kenyatta knew that such patronage did not necessarily make an African a committed Communist.

But both the Europeans and Indians of Kenya feared that if Odinga's influence prevailed in Kenyatta's new cabinet, the country might follow the lines of a Red police state with land and property confiscation.

The new Prime Minister recognized that he needed both men and the following they commanded. But trusting neither, he adroitly played one off against the other. Each was given the cabinet post that the other wanted. Denying authority to Tom Mboya to shape the new direction of Kenya's economy, he appointed him Minister for Justice. Withholding police powers from Oginga Odinga, Kenyatta made him Minister for Home Affairs. It was a perfect standoff.

James Gichuru, a fellow Kikuyu, became Finance Minister. Other cabinet posts were distributed with an eye toward representation of Kenya's other tribes.

Kenyatta was determined to avoid the kind of tribal rivalry that had torn apart the Congo after it had won independence from Belgium, forcing the UN to intervene to restore order. The best way to save Kenya from a similar fate, he knew, was to create a strong central government. So he sought to modify the constitution to strengthen his government's powers, especially over the police and civil service. To win tribal support, he assured each tribe of a share of power in the decisions of the new government.

"If this country of ours is to prosper," he told black and white Kenyans, "we must create a sense of togetherness, of national familyhood. In Swahili, we express this by the word *ujamaa,* which can also be roughly translated as socialism. We must bring all the communities of Kenya together, to build a unified nation. . . . Where there has been tribal animosity, it will be finished. Let us not dwell upon the bitterness of the past. I would rather look to the future, to the good new Kenya, not to the bad old days."

Recognizing the need for a large corps of college-educated Africans to develop this "good new Kenya," he encouraged an emigration of the nation's most intelligent young people to seek higher education in Europe and America.

Some African politicians in Parliament accused him of sending away the flower of Kenya's youth to be indoctrinated by the poisons of Western white racism. Why had he not, instead, encouraged them to be trained in Ghana, Egypt or in other African countries? He replied in Parliament.

"Brothers," he said, "I want to assure you that knowledge is knowledge, irrespective of who gives it. You must make a distinction between knowledge and ideology. We do not send our people overseas to get the ideology of Britain or America or Russia. We send them to get knowledge, to come back to this country to help us work for our future."

He prepared to take Kenya into the United Nations as soon as he could compel Britain to grant official independence. Meanwhile he asked for and received thirty-two UN specialists to help develop the country's economy, agriculture, irrigation projects, cooperatives, health and school services.

"What we are trying to achieve here," he told them in a speech of welcome in Nairobi, "is a step toward that ideal of a free and united world which the United Nations is striving to bring about."

Over and over again he made it clear to the country that although he was a Kikuyu, his tribe would be shown absolutely no favoritism. It was a tribute to the esteem in which he was held that he was the one Kenyan trusted by all tribes to be just to all and to keep them at peace.

"I am not just a Prime Minister for the Kikuyu," he declared in a speech at the Mombasa Stadium. "Whether you are a Kikuyu or a member of another tribe is beside the point. My work is essentially for the African people, and I have no room for tribalists in my heart." He hoped that the final struggle for independence would unite Kenya's tribes and help prepare them to work together as a modern nation.

Through Mboya he gradually restructured the federal powers that the British, using KADU, had deliberately fractured and divided among Kenya's seven tribal regions. In a broadcast he said, "If we can create this sense of national direction and identity, we shall have gone a long way toward solving our economic problems. We hold out no empty promises of achieving utopia overnight. What we hold out to every citizen is the prospect of work, justly rewarded."

Uhuru was already assured in the near future. He began stumping the country with a new slogan, one he hoped would become an even greater inspiration. It was summed up in a Swahili exhortation used by African tree-loggers and meaning, "Let's all pull together."

"*Harambee!*" he shouted to enthusiastic crowds.

"*Harambee!*" they roared back loyally.

But it was going to take more than a slogan, Kenyatta knew, to operate an Africanized Kenya with the efficiency and resources of the colonial government it was replacing.

The economy of Kenya depended on the prosperity of the 56,000 wealthy white settlers who now produced 80 percent of Kenya's cash crops and were responsible for 70 percent of the country's foreign exchange earnings. It was only white cooperation, too, that could provide black jobs.

Even now Kenya's unemployment rate was a high 20 percent, and growing worse because of a population explosion. The African population of Kenya, UN experts warned Kenyatta, could be expected to double by 1980. On top of all his other problems, he was in a desperate race against time.

His chief dilemma lay in the fact that the white settlers he had fought most of his life, who feared and hated him for overthrowing their way of life and who still blamed him for Mau Mau, felt unwilling to entrust their fortunes in his hands. They steadily cut back their investments and switched out of crops that required extensive hand labor, like tea and coffee, to barley and wheat. African farm laborers by the thousands were thrown out of work.

Some 80,000 jobless now squatted on the white settlers' lands, refusing to leave because they had nowhere to go.

A crippling flight of capital and a halt to industrial investment had also left about 320,000 jobless in the cities.

The treasury, deprived of revenues, was almost empty. There was grave danger, too, that once the British troops left, civil war might break out between rival tribes in a fight for British lands. Some of Kenyatta's ministers urged him to postpone pressure for independence until after some of these dangerous problems had first been solved.

Kenyatta refused. He and Kenya had already waited too long for freedom, no matter what chaos and difficulties freedom brought in its wake. He was going to be seventy-four. Now only a few years at best could remain to him to achieve his lifelong dream of a Republic of Kenya. He felt the expectations of millions of Africans like a great weight upon his shoulders. Those who mattered most to him were the younger generation, to whom he wished to bequeath a free nation so that they could feel a new national pride and purpose.

Perhaps he had dreamed the impossible dream.

But, somehow, he had to make it come true.

12

A Nation Is Freed

KENYATTA'S HOPES WERE UNASHAMEDLY BUILT ON THE economic foundation the white settlers had built for themselves with African labor—schools, railroad, ports, hospitals, roads, communications, public utilities, cultivated rich farmlands and a modern civil service. He was passionately determined that these facilities would provide the same good life for Africans that they had for the white settlers.

But he was also realist enough to recognize that his untrained people were not yet ready to manage this complex economy on their own. To buy the time he needed to make the Republic of Kenya work after *Uhuru*, he had to convince the white settlers that he was not really their enemy.

Thirty thousand Kikuyu had once cheered him wildly when he shouted, "We want self-government. Don't be afraid to spill your blood to get the land!" But now he had to turn around and tell his people to be patient, to continue enduring hardship and injustice in order to keep the economy from collapsing. He would have to offer the Europeans solid guarantees of protection to persuade them to keep their skills and capital in Kenya for at least another decade.

On August 12, 1963, he created a sensation by appearing personally at the Nakuru Town Hall before a gathering of hundreds of European farmers and their wives. These white citizens stared in stolid fascination at their black Prime Minister as he walked to the front of the stage, fly whisk over one shoulder. Leaning on his walking stick, he began talking to them in a quiet voice.

"We want you to stay and to farm well in this country," he told them. "That is the policy of this government. What the government needs is experience, and I don't care where it comes from: I will take it with both hands. Continue to farm your land well, and you will get all the encouragement and protection of the government."

"What about our stock thefts?" one settler shouted.

"The government will do everything possible to stop such crimes." Then his voice grew husky with emotion. "We can all work together harmoniously to make this country great, and to show other countries in the world that different racial groups can live and work together. Become Africans in your hearts, and we will welcome you with open arms!"

In a moment of inspiration, he swung his fly whisk and called out his Swahili slogan urging cooperation:

"Harambee!"

There was a moment of stunned silence. He waited tensely for a reaction to the appeal he had couched in unmistakably black African terms. He cried again: *"Harambee!"*

Weatherbeaten white farmers in his audience stared at each other in a state of cultural shock. His husky voice rang out at them a third time in a heartfelt cry for their hand in partnership: *"Harambee!"*

If his listeners remained icily silent, he knew there would be no hope for an integrated free Kenya. He would have had his answer from the white community. With tremendous personal courage, he had sought that answer openly, laying himself open to a humiliating rebuff in public.

Then a handful of Europeans, moved, sprang to their feet. Sweeping aside the color barrier that divided Kenya into black and white, they waved their arms and shouted back enthusiastically: *"Harambee! Harambee!"* Their outbursts touched off others, like firecrackers. Soon almost every settler in the hall, overcoming his white British reserve, was on his feet joining in the cry. The hall became the scene of a spontaneous ceremony of racial reconciliation.

Tears of joy glistened in the old African's eyes.

The white man had finally seen past his black skin, and understood what was in his heart. The old enmity between them was dead. Now they were all simply Africans together, black and white, who loved the special country they held in common. Instead of fighting over Kenya, now they could join together in working for it and sharing it.

Word of the meeting at Nakuru spread like wildfire.

Settlers who loved their land too much to leave it felt hopeful. They knew that when the British flag was hauled down in Kenya, only one man would be able to protect their lives and homes—Jomo Kenyatta, the African who now asked them to trust him. Many did, feeling that he was proving himself to be a strong, wise and moderate statesman.

But for many others he was still the evil genius of Mau Mau, the "leader of his people to darkness and death" that Governor Renison had branded him. Strongly biased racially, distrustful of black rule, they would have nothing to do with *Harambee*.

They began leaving Kenya at the rate of 600 a month.

Independence Day was set for December 11, 1963. Official ceremonies transferring power from Great Britain to the new Republic of Kenya were scheduled at Nairobi's newly named Uhuru Stadium near one of Kenya's famous game parks.

As preparations for the great day went forward, news reached Kenya of a dramatic assassination in Dallas, Texas. Jomo Kenyatta was stunned and grieved. President John F. Kennedy had been a true friend of Kenya. Until Kennedy had reached the White House, Kenyatta felt, the United States had behaved like any other imperialist power, with little sympathy for nations struggling against colonialism.

Under the Eisenhower Administration, Secretary of State John Foster Dulles had denied foreign aid to underdeveloped countries unwilling to support the United States in the Cold War. Those that insisted upon their sovereign right to a neutral, independent foreign policy were suspect as "Communist."

In 1960, African students in Kenya had been granted scholarships by sympathetic American universities. They could not accept them, however, because they were too poor to afford the fare to the United States. A request for assistance had been made to the State Department—in vain.

Senator John Kennedy, then Chairman of the African Subcommittee of the Senate Foreign Relations Committee, had been indignant at this lack of sympathy for the poverty of an African nation struggling for educational assistance. Through the Kennedy Foundation he had arranged for a special goodwill airlift to bring the students to America.

When Kennedy became President, his first State Department appointment was G. Mennen Williams as Assistant Secretary for African Affairs. Visiting Nairobi, Williams observed publicly that Africa ought to be for the Africans. The British Foreign Office filed an indignant protest to Washington. Asked by the press to comment, Kennedy had shrugged, "Well, I don't know who *else* Africa should be for!

When it became clear that Jomo Kenyatta was winning his struggle for Kenya's independence, President Kennedy had asked Congress to reverse the Dulles policy and offer United States aid without strings to the emerging new republic.

Understandably, his death saddened Kenyatta, who delivered a stirring tribute to the fallen American President in Kenya's House of Representatives. Praising John Kennedy as a great American, he nevertheless did not hesitate to criticize America itself as a racist society.

"President Kennedy became in the eyes of the Negroes another Lincoln," Kenyatta declared. "He spoke out for civil rights, and challenged the conscience of the American people . . . the biggest challenge that American bigotry and racial hypocrisy has every faced."

He added, "We in Kenya have an additional special reason to remember him . . . his generous interest in assisting our young boys and girls to study in America through the student airlift. The world has lost a great man."

When *Uhuru* Day came at last, it ushered in a three-day public holiday. Nairobi seemed to burst at the seams as hundreds of thousands of Kenyans massed into the city from all over the country. There were Turkana tribesmen from the northwest desert, Luo warriors from Lake Victoria in the west, tall Masai spearmen from the southern border, turbaned Arabs from the humid Coastal Strip in the east.

Samburu women had walked sixty miles a day south from frontier scrublands. Kipsigis squatters came down from the White Highlands, mingling with Taita tribesmen who lived in the shadow of Mount Kilimanjaro on the Tanganyika border.

No Africans caused more commotion than two-thousand tattered Mau Mau who emerged from forests where they had been hiding for ten years. They had refused to trust the British proclamation of 1960 ending the state of emergency; nor had they felt safe even when Jomo Kenyatta became Prime Minister.

It was only when he had declared a general political amnesty, acknowledging the Mau Mau as patriots, that they were willing to lay down their arms and leave the forests. Now, clutching invitations to occupy a place of honor at the *Uhuru* Day ceremonies, they made their way proudly to Nairobi. They felt confident that *Mzee* would grant the reward they expected—two thousand farm plots in the Highlands.

Most were hard-core Mau Mau, the old thugs from Nairobi who had turned the KCA resistance into a criminal operation. Many arrived drunk on *Uhuru* beer. Hearing they would be coming, many frightened whites who had planned to attend the ceremonies stayed home instead. Kenyatta was criticized by both Africans and whites for having dignified the Mau Mau cause he had so often insisted he opposed.

"How could I refuse recognition to the Land Freedom Army?" he pointed out. "*All* Mau Mau should not be blamed for the crimes of a minority. Besides, we must all put the past behind us. We must have every group with us for *Harambee*."

144

Recognition, he felt, was the quickest way to end the nuisance of the Mau Mau. He hoped to appease them by offering public honors in lieu of land. To win British cooperation, he had agreed that after independence, only 250,000 acres a year could be purchased in the White Highlands for Africans. First claim on this land, moreover, had to go to tribesmen native to the region. Kenyatta hoped that before the Mau Mau learned of this pact their emergence into the open and dispersion would prevent any retreat to the forests to stir up trouble for the new republic.

Independence Stadium overflowed with humanity. Outside tens of thousands more Africans milled around listening to the celebration through loudspeakers. Tribal music, ceremonies and dances lasted through most of the day. A glittering audience of distinguished guests, including Britain's Prince Philip and U. S. Secretary of the Interior Stewart Udall, looked on. When darkness fell, the stadium was brilliantly lit by eighty blazing floodlights.

Exactly at midnight the lights suddenly went out, plunging the great crowds into darkness except for an orange African moon. There was a solemn hush as the Union Jack that had flown over Kenya since 1895 was hauled down and removed from the flagstaff. It was Kenyatta who had ordered this ceremony performed in darkness, to spare British settlers the anguish of watching their flag lowered.

Then the floodlights came back on again. The crowds roared as the new black, red and green flag of the independent Republic of Kenya soared upward in a blaze of light.

"*Uhuru! Uhuru!*" The crowds went wild with joy as fireworks exploded in the African sky. The band of the Kenya Rifles, wearing caps of *Colobus* monkey skin, struck up the opening bars of Kenya's new national anthem, *Eee Mungu Nguvu Yetu* (O God of All Creation).

Governor Malcolm MacDonald, newly accredited to Kenya by the British Commonwealth, rose to swear in the country's first President. Every eye was fixed on the bearded old African who now came forward, the familiar fly whisk over his shoulder like a burlesque mace. After being sworn into office, he made the expected polite speech in English.

Then, pausing, he gazed around at his people with a wry, warm smile, and spoke out to them spontaneously in Swahili. They listened in spellbound silence, drinking in every word.

All Africans in Kenya were grateful to Britain, he declared, for bowing at last to their demand for independence. Now that they were out from under the British thumb, the two nations could clasp hands in voluntary friendship. He acknowledged freely that his new government would probably make mistakes, asking understanding and forgiveness from any—"black, white or brown"—who might suffer because of them.

He reminded his people that although Kenya would now taste "the honey of *Uhuru*," there were still other African brothers being exploited by white colonialism—principally in South Africa, Mozambique and Angola. He urged them to support his cooperation with other free African nations to end all colonialism on the African continent. "If we achieve unity," he declared, "the whole world will respect us."

Foreign diplomats as well as Kenya politicians perked with interest as he declared his intention to answer those who predicted his orientation toward Moscow or Washington.

"I want all those nations who are present today—whether from West or from East—to understand our aim," he declared, lapsing into English. "We want to befriend all, and we want aid from everyone. But we do *not* want assistance from any person or country who will say: 'Kenyatta, if you want aid, you must agree to this or that.' "

In Swahili he continued, "I believe, my brothers, and I tell you now, that it is better to be poor and remain free, than to be technically free but still kept on a string. A horse cannot choose: reins can be put on him so he can be led around as his owner desires. We will *not* be prepared to accept any aid that will tie us like a horse by its reins!"

He cautioned his people not to expect that *Uhuru* would bring them an automatic paradise. "I tell you there will be nothing from Heaven," he warned, brandishing his fly whisk derisively at the sky. "We must all work hard, with our hands, to save ourselves from poverty, ignorance and disease. We ourselves can save us—but nobody else!" Disaster would overtake them, he prophesied, if they simply fell asleep under a mango or coconut tree, praying to God that fruit would fall down beside them while they dozed in the sun.

Addressing the hard-core Mau Mau, he snapped, 'Do not think that because there is no longer a colonial government, there will no longer be need to respect the country's laws. The laws of the country will remain; the police and prisons will remain. Do not think that, because the other day I freed about eight thousand people from prison, all prison doors will be closed and no more people will be sent in!"

Toward the end of his electrifying speech, he called for a show of hands from all Africans willing to help him build their nation and obey its laws. A forest of hands waved enthusiastically. He beamed in delight. Encouraged, he pointed out that in the past they had been able to blame the Europeans for everything that went wrong in Kenya. Unable to build enough of their own schools, they had blamed the Europeans for educating European children and the Asians for educating Asian children. Jealousy was not enough.

"Now the government is ours," he challenged, "Maybe you will now be blaming Kenyatta, saying, 'Kenyatta, we elected you, but where is this or that?' But you must know that Kenyatta alone cannot give you everything. All things we must do together . . . to develop our country, to get education for our children, to have doctors, to build roads."

He roared out at them the answer: *"Harambee!"*

"HARAMBEE!" they thundered back.

But the notables present wondered whether determination alone, even with a dynamic leader like Jomo Kenyatta, would be enough. The terrible fate of the Congo, which had fallen into turmoil with independence, was the unmentioned specter at the feast. Only a week earlier, too, three provinces of the Sudan had revolted. Besides tribalism, Kenyatta had to cope with poverty, illiteracy and disease, which he himself called the greatest enemies of his country.

Kenya's white settlers waited, many apprehensively, for the first significant acts of the new republic. They were not greatly reassured when the statue of Lord Delamere, Kenya's first white settler, was torn off its pedestal in Nairobi's main intersection. Rumor had it that the new statue replacing it would glorify Dedan Kemathi, a Mau Mau leader hanged by the British in 1957 for strangling loyal Africans.

Kenya's 176,000 Asians, who operated most of the

shops and controlled marketing, distribution and transportation, were also apprehensive. They were more easily replaced by Africans, they knew, than the British. Hundreds began to queue up daily in Nairobi to apply for British passports, in order to be able to leave Kenya quickly if trouble arose.

But Kenyatta's major preoccupation was keeping tribal rivalries from blowing the new republic apart. Although KANU had a three-to-one majority in Parliament, it represented primarily only the three largest tribes— Kikuyu, Luo and Kamba. KADU represented some forty different minority tribes, many seriously discontented.

The first challenge to *Harambee* came from 200,000 Somalis of the Northeastern Region. They had boycotted the general elections, insisting upon their right to secede from Kenya and join tribal kin in neighboring Somalia. More was at stake than just the Northeastern Region.

A civil war at the very outset of his new country's life, Kenyatta knew, could prove fatal. Yet if he allowed the Somalis to succeed, he would open the door to other demands for separation by other tribes, leading to tribal warfare. White settlers would not wait for all of Kenya to dissolve into chaos like the Congo. They would abandon the farms on which the nation depended for its wealth, and the republic would be shattered.

Kenyatta spent hours alone wrestling with the problem, which had become involved in the Cold War struggle for influence in Africa. The Soviet Union had concluded a $26 million arms deal with the Somalia Government, which now announced that it was increasing its army. Somalia guerrillas tested Kenyan resistance by "unofficial" raids on border police posts.

To oppose a full-scale Somalia invasion Kenyatta could count only on three well-trained battalions of Kenya Rifles and 4,500 British troops scheduled to be withdrawn in eighteen months. Kenyatta nervously informed British officials in London that he was willing to sign a five-year military aid agreement to keep British troops on Kenya soil.

The British agreed, enjoying the irony. But there was even greater irony in a mutiny by Kenya's own black troops.

13 ‹‹‹‹‹‹‹‹‹‹‹‹‹‹‹‹‹

"Harambee!"

THE TROUBLE BROKE OUT AT LANET CAMP, SIXTY MILES from Nairobi. Freed of colonial control, the African 11th Battalion of the Kenya Army suddenly mutinied, demanding higher wages and promotions to jobs held by white officers. Coming so swiftly after independence, the revolt was a stunning blow to Kenyatta's authority and prestige.

The mutiny had been inspired by a similar rebellion in neighboring Tanganyika to the south. President Julius Nyerere's government had almost been overthrown until Nyerere, in desperation, had requested British military help.

Kenyatta showed a firm face to the rebels. Refusing to bargain with them, he announced tersely that leaders of the mutiny would be court-martialed. Like Nyerere, he was compelled to swallow his pride and ask the commander of the British garrison to put down the revolt. The alternative was the risk of a military coup that could overthrow the republic and establish an army dictatorship.

At the same time he knew the importance of being a flexible leader, responsive to protest. The British had lost Kenya to him because the colonial government had

151

remained rigid and unmoved in the face of popular unrest.

So even while he moved to uphold the republic's authority, he promised to investigate army grievances and redress those found to be genuine. "We shall press on with the program of Africanization," he declared, "and I hope that most of the top officer and executive posts will be held by Africans within this year."

Some of his ministers also urged him to ask the British to send forces to the Somalia border to deal with raids by Somali gangs called *shifta*. But Kenyatta hesitated. He knew that many of the Somali who would be killed would be sympathizers who were Kenya nationals.

On February 26, 1964, he went to Parliament and openly addressed the Somali members who represented the country's North-Eastern Region. "We know that many of you are herdsmen during the day and *shifta* at night, while others conceal *shifta*," he told them. "We are faced with a very grave situation. Some people in the House would applaud loudly if I said I would issue orders for the Army to shoot on sight."

There was a burst of applause. Kenyatta shook his head. "But this I will not do, because we are human beings, and sometimes—whether we are angry or not—we must act as human beings. This is not the way to settle problems; you cannot settle problems by shooting. I consider the Somali in the North-Eastern Region as our brothers. You have to negotiate with your brothers; you have to talk to them."

Then he told the House his decision—to turn the problem over to the Organization of African Unity, relying on the pressure of the thirty-two nations joined in OAU to compel Somalia to keep the peace.

His troubles were only beginning. At a KANU

Youth Conference, Oginga Odinga maneuvered behind the scenes to win a resolution calling upon Kenyatta to move promptly to introduce socialism into the republic. The Conference called for an all-out nationalization program—confiscation of all white settler lands and Asian businesses, and even the expulsion from Kenya of all but black Africans.

China's Chou En-lai, touring Africa in February, told reporters in obvious delight, "Revolutionary prospects are excellent throughout Africa." Kenyatta angrily withdrew an official invitation that had been extended to the Red Chinese leader to visit Nairobi.

"Kenya intends to avert all revolutions, irrespective of their origins," he snapped. Soon afterward he ordered the deportation of a Red Chinese journalist found to be involved in dealings with Kenya politicians. When a team of Russian military advisers sought to stay in Kenya longer than Kenyatta deemed prudent, he also sent them packing.

Storm clouds continued to pile up over his fledgling republic. He was aware of rising murmurs of discontent on all sides as problems multiplied. The foreign press reported that his popularity was threatened, his prestige and authority in question. Some correspondents wrote that the realities of responsibility were too much for him. Others that he had made too many promises, raised too many false hopes.

"The sad conviction here," reported the Nairobi correspondent for the London *Times,* "is that Mr. Kenyatta has basically lost control of Kenya."

Harassed but determined to preserve the republic, Kenyatta sought to reinspire his people by launching bold new plans for the country's development. He instituted a community self-help program that encouraged the people themselves, with government aid, to build the new schools, clinics and roads they needed. A Youth Brigade was organized to create work for idle youths in town and country.

He developed a crash program to provide 50,000 new jobs in just a few months. Farmers and factory owners were required to increase their payrolls by 10 percent, in exchange for two concessions—a wage freeze by labor unions, and resettlement of unwanted squatters on white settler farms.

To satisfy his people's cry for land, Kenyatta sent his cabinet ministers on a tour of Western capitals to borrow $300 million for buying or leasing more land in the Highlands. He rejected coldly Odinga's suggestion of a "Republic Lands Ordinance" that would nullify the old Crown Lands Ordinance and "take back" the farmlands of white settlers.

He sought to strengthen Kenya's economic position by joining with Tanzania and Uganda in a Federation of East Africa. The three former British colonies, covering an area almost the size of western Europe, already shared a common currency, customs, postal system and railways. In time, Kenyatta hoped, they could do for each other what the Common Market had done for the nations of western Europe.

Odinga disapproved, regarding the new Federation as Western-oriented. Kenyatta was angered when he learned that Odinga, behind his back, was trying to muster enough votes in Parliament to defeat the FEA plan. Using his personal popularity with the members, he easily won ratification for it. Odinga beat a sullen retreat to wait for a more opportune time to challenge the leadership of *Mzee*.

When Kenyatta had steered his weak and troubled

republic safely through the shoals of the first few months, he turned his efforts to urging his people, through hard work, to leap from a stone age culture into the twentieth century in a single decade. It was a staggering objective.

"Now that we have *Uhuru,* the next thing is to build the nation," he told *Newsweek* correspondent John P. Nugent. "Now I must see the progress, see the standard of living raised." Half-closing his eyes dreamily as his grandfather Kongo had done when peering mystically into the future, he murmured to himself as though beholding a vision, "Yaas, yaas, yaas . . ."

Jealous rivals observed dryly that *Mzee's* rise to power had certainly raised his own standard of living. Gone were the lumber jacket and sandals of revolutionary and prison days, replaced by a blue chalk-stripe suit with Western tie, a gold ring, a fly whisk with a silver handle.

Instead of the old motorcycle with which he had once roared out to the reserves after work as a KCA agitator, now he drove a Mercedes, Lincoln convertible and Rolls Royce. But to reaffirm his identity as an African tribesman he still wore his old beaded *kenyatta* belt and a Luo beaded hat, and carried his chief's walking stick with a carved elephant head.

He made weekend trips into the countryside to visit villages and encourage the self-help program by inspecting the schools, clinics and roads under construction. Exhorting villagers to work even harder, longer and faster, he would scold them for whatever shortcomings he had heard about people of that district—drinking, stealing cattle from white settlers, vandalism, starting tribal fights.

He urged them not to listen to any leaders who en-

155

couraged them to do bad things out of hate and spite.

"Do you want to be run by drunkards?" he would roar.

"No, *Mzee!*" the villagers shouted back.

"By womanizers? By corrupt men?"

"No, no, *Mzee!*"

"By whom, then? By whom?"

"Kenyatta! Kenyatta!"

"Harambee!"

"Harambee!"

Then off he would speed to the next village to repeat his inspirational message. He loved best to drive up new roads winding through clusters of mud-and-wattle huts to new schoolhouses built on hilltops. Thrilled teachers would proudly order class recitations—not just in their own tribal language, but also in the pan-African language of Swahili and the international language of English.

Kenyatta would beam. The new generation, he was determined, must grow up with the communication skills necessary to make the Republic of Kenya part of the modern world community.

Driving over the cool, rolling hills of the Highlands, he inspected the small farms now being worked by a thousand Africans who had been given government loans to buy land from the white settlers. The beautiful, spacious lawns and flower gardens had been sacrificed to essential crops of corn and beans—not only enough to keep a family alive, but a surplus to sell. The farms were flourishing, Kenyatta noted in satisfaction, thanks to modern techniques taught by the UN agricultural teams.

If only he could give the same opportunities to the 30,000 African squatters living unwanted on the big European plantations! These landless families, many with up to ten children apiece to feed, were bitter and hostile.

They stole crops and cattle, often vindictively poisoning or damaging what they could not steal. Many white settlers, exasperated by Kenyatta's reluctance to use troops or police to move the squatters off, were trying to sell out and leave.

It was useless moving the squatters off, Kenyatta knew, because they always drifted back. There was simply no place else for them to go. He waited hopefully for his emissaries to return from abroad with new loans he could use to buy up more Highlands plantations to divide among the squatters.

"We could requisition the land," one minister hinted, "and pay the owners in bonds redeemable in thirty years."

"Be honest and call it confiscation!" Kenyatta snapped. "After that how many Europeans or Americans would want to make investments in Kenya? They won't have any faith in our future unless we're willing to solve our problems by our own hard work. If my own ministers can't understand that, how can I ever get it through the heads of my people?"

He worried, besides, about antagonizing the remaining white settlers, whom he depended upon to avoid famine and to sustain Kenya's earnings from agricultural exports. Eventually, he knew, most would leave, but he hoped to make their departure slow, gradual and nondisruptive. He needed at the very least a five-year period of transition.

But the land problem was causing severe unrest among the desperate squatters. Reports reached Kenyatta of a resurgence of Mau Mau. Under the guise of a new secret society called the Weeping Kamau, it was recruiting squatters in the Aberdares. There were rumors once more of terrible oathings, floggings of Africans who resisted the oath, raids on European farms to steal food.

Old Mau Mau beaded headdresses were glimpsed in forest hideouts. It was all too painfully familiar. This time Kenyatta did not equivocate.

Speeding off to a tour of the disaffected area, he used his personal prestige and eloquence to crush support for this attempt to revive Mau Mau savagery.

"Some people have been disseminating malicious propaganda," he warned crowds of squatters, "saying that all this land will be distributed freely. But I say that no one will be allowed to take land when he likes. You must use *only* the land which has been allocated to you. More and more will be made available as we are able to afford to buy it."

Knowing that witch doctors were a mainstay of Mau Mau, he sought to shake the superstitious regard in which they were held. "If you see a witch doctor, you will undoubtedly find that he is poor," he pointed out. "If he says he will make you rich, ask why he is not rich himself!" The true way for a family to prosper, he urged, was to do everything possible to see to it that their children were educated.

"There are people who go about telling others to return to the forests," he said grimly. "These people who go into the forests and feed on stolen things, are they not vagabonds? . . . We took oaths to regain our freedom. But if people ask you to take oaths now, it will be oaths against *your* government—and therefore against *yourselves!*"

Returning to Nairobi, Kenyatta learned that one of his trusted assistants, Bildad Kaggia, the militant, thick-bearded Kikuyu with flashing eyes who had been one of his five co-defendants in the Mau Mau trial, had been chiefly responsible for secret agitation of the landless squatters in the Rift Valley on behalf of the new Mau Mau movement.

158

Kenyatta promptly fired Kaggia, who sullenly muttered that *Mzee* would rue the day. Afterward Kenyatta, shaking his gray beard, sighed to Gichuru, "There are some of our people who simply don't know what it means to be a Kenyan first, an African next and Kikuyu last!"

Without the blunders of a colonial government to keep it going, the new threat of Mau Mau limped into oblivion.

Since Kenya, while free, was still a voluntary member of the British Commonwealth, Kenyatta found himself under pressure from London to support the West in the Cold War struggle with the Soviet Union. On July 8, 1964, he flew to London to attend the Commonwealth Prime Ministers Conference, where he bluntly laid his cards on the table.

"I made it clear that Kenya follows a policy of nonalignment in world affairs," he reported back to the Kenya Parliament. "Countries committed to the West should fully accept that Kenya does not have to agree to or approve their conduct in the Cold War." He was not simply being cynical, like Nasser, in seeking the highest bid for his favor.

"We want help from *all* quarters," he told the press. "What we *don't* want is what we call in Swahili a *Bwana Kubwa*—a master. We want friends. Those who want to be masters must find somewhere elsc. We have no place for them."

The new American President, Lyndon B. Johnson, chose to support the policy of his assassinated predecessor by providing aid to Kenya while respecting Kenyatta's right to remain neutral in the Cold War. Kenya was granted United States economic and technical assistance worth $3 million annually, plus another half million a year in development loans. American aid also helped develop a Kenya National Youth Service and a Kenya National Police Air Wing.

Oginga Odinga viewed such United States aid darkly, especially when it was followed by American investments totaling $80 million in Nairobi firms. To Odinga, no matter how much Kenyatta protested his neutrality, the facts added up to sizable American influence in the Republic of Kenya. Did not such economic penetration represent American imperialism every bit as sordid and oppressive as Britain's colonial control of Kenya had been?

Stung by his criticism, Kenyatta answered in Parliament. "I must warn those in our country who seek to create confusion. It is true that we have passed through many years of Western imperialism. It is natural that we should detest Western colonialism, and associate the word 'imperialism' with the West." Then his voice pulsed with conviction.

"But if we are *truly* nonaligned, we must not avoid making friends with those Western countries which extend an honest field of cooperation and trade. To do this is just to prove that we are *not* free, and cannot separate good from bad. It proves that we still suffer from a colonial mentality!"

Odinga remained sullenly unconvinced. But those who knew Kenyatta best felt that Odinga was wrong. So was the United States if it imagined that it had bought him.

"Don't be fooled," one of his cabinet ministers tipped off a reporter confidentially. *"Mzee* was an African nationalist in the days of Mau Mau and he still is. He does not stand in East or West, even if it seems that way. He stands in Africa with both feet, and he cares for the people of Africa as he does for his own children."

160

Even with his hands full of the pressures of nation-building, Kenyatta did not forget fellow Africans who were still living in colonial bondage. He joined other African leaders in pressuring the British Commonwealth and the UN to boycott South Africa for its apartheid policies.

"Our freedom will be useless," he warned Kenyans at a giant rally in Nairobi on June 21, 1964, "if our brothers continue to be enslaved in South Africa." The West came in for scathing criticism: "Britain and the United States in particular pay lip-service to our cause, while they go on underpinning the South African economy by their investments, their buying and their sales. And it is critics in *those* countries who are stupid enough to accuse *us* of bringing the Cold War to Africa, when we declare our readiness to accept aid in our struggle from other sources!"

He pointed up the mistake of the West in not supporting African freedom and free choice. "By refusing to participate in workable sanctions against South Africa, the countries of the West are creating a situation in which violence becomes the only answer. If, by their neglect to take nonviolent measures, there are fighting and bloodshed, where will the countries of the West stand *then?*"

Many of the ministers in his cabinet, and members of Kenya's Parliament, wondered how *Mzee,* at seventy-four, could stand up to the pressure of so many vexing problems tumbling over his weary shoulders. "You really should rest more," one of his followers urged anxiously, "and let some of the younger men carry some of your burden."

Kenyatta smiled disdainfully. "Nonsense! There is nothing a man of forty can do that I cannot!" Sensing a subtle hint that he was growing too old for office, and ought to step down for either Mboya or Odinga, he added testily, "I don't play a second fiddle. I wouldn't do that. I feel I am controlling the party, and I'm capable of doing it."

Neither Mboya nor Odinga was happy to hear it.

14 ‹‹‹‹‹‹‹‹‹‹‹‹‹‹‹‹‹

Challenge to the Lion

KENYATTA DEMONSTRATED HIS VIGOR AND WILINESS AS A powerful political boss by persuading Ronald Ngala of KADU, leader of the opposition, to join KANU, turning Kenya into a one-party state. He convinced Ngala that a parliamentary form of government was not necessarily best for an emerging nation. What Kenya needed, he insisted, was forceful leadership to guide it through the early years of independence.

Ngala needed no more conviction than the frightening example of the Congo that tribal conflict could plunge a nation freed from colonialism into a devastating civil war. Ngala's alarmed supporters warned, "*Mzee* wants to be a dicatator!" But Ngala knew this fear was unwarranted. So on November 10, 1964, he voluntarily dissolved KADU and announced that henceforth all members of his parliamentary group would cooperate with the government, under the political leadership of *Mzee* Kenyatta, in a trusting spirit of national unity.

This remarkable tribute to Kenyatta marked the end of the struggle between the minority tribal leaders, represented by KADU, and the central government, represented by KANU. Kenyatta was deeply moved.

Now, he told Parliament in relief, the energies of *all*

Kenyans could be turned solidly toward nation-building. No one need fear dictatorship. He would always provide full opportunity for debate and opposition. But time and energy need no longer be wasted on political opposition for the sake of opposition. Nor would tribal rivalries be allowed to flourish and tear the nation apart senselessly.

But there was more to Kenyatta's political triumph in eliminating KADU as a political force than just a consolidation of power for *Harambee*. As long as KADU remained a legal opposition, he knew, it would be tempted into secret alliances with East or West in the hope of regaining power through foreign arms and money. It was the British, after all, who had financed and built up KADU originally.

In the Congo the Western powers had backed one faction, the Communist powers the other, with the result that the Congo Republic had been torn apart in a Cold War struggle. Kenyatta was determined that this would not happen to Kenya.

At the same time, he wanted the West to understand that his reason for forging a one-party state did not in any way imply either a turning toward Communist dictatorship or a new policy of hostility toward the democracies.

"We reject a blueprint of the Western model of a two-party system of government," he explained in a public speech aimed at Washington and London, "because we do not subscribe to the notion of the government and the governed being in opposition to one another, one clamoring for duties and the other crying for rights."

He reassured the West that his new one-party system was not based on the Marxist idea of parties representing social classes. "The theory of class struggle has no relevance to our particular situation here. In a one-party state such as we envisage, we hold that politics is a potent instrument; it is through our political institutions that we influence economic trends, not the other way around."

In December, when the Republic of Kenya was one year old, he invited a special guest from London to attend the Independence Day birthday celebration. Old memories stirred in *Mzee's* breast as he clasped the hands of Edna Grace Clark Kenyatta, the white third wife he had left behind in London almost twenty years before with his life as a European, rather than subject her to the indignities she would have had to face under the colonial color bar.

Now she sat on the platform as his guest of honor, listening to huge crowds roar their affection for the husband she still legally shared with three African wives. Kenyatta learned from Edna that their son was attending Cambridge. A radical Socialist, Peter Kenyatta hoped to come to Africa to enter Kenya politics.

"We will need him," Kenyatta assured her. "We need every educated son of Africans to help build our nation."

Although he had closed the door to foreign meddling in the affairs of Kenya, Kenyatta still had to deal with powerful pro-Communist forces within the country. Their spokesman in the cabinet was Oginga Odinga. He openly supported Bildad Kaggia, whom Kenyatta had kicked out of office for trying to revive Mau Mau against the white settlers.

Kaggia was operating a school called the Lumumba Institute, named after the assassinated Congo leader who had been backed by the Communist powers. Moscow-financed and staffed by a faculty of two Russians and eight Moscow-trained Africans, the school provided Marxist courses for KANU party officials. Great emphasis was laid on leaders who developed into "dictators removed from the people who elected them."

Kaggia's personal following included landless Kikuyu squatters and left-wing students of the University of East Africa in Nairobi (formerly the Royal College).

Kenyatta suddenly padlocked the Lumumba Institute.

"I know about communism," he growled. "I've seen it, and cannot be fooled. I know how it works!"

He was making it clear to Moscow and Peking that because he had slammed the doors of Kenya in the face of Western imperialists did not mean that he was opening the country's back doors to Communist infiltration.

Moving to cut off Kaggia from popular support, he called a mass meeting in Nairobi. Tens of thousands of Africans listened thoughtfully as he warned them against Communist-paid countrymen who tried to persuade them to follow foreign Red banners. A Red regime in Kenya, he told them, would curtail their freedom just as much as colonialism had done.

"This is why we reject communism," he declared. "It is in fact the reason why we have chosen for ourselves the policy of nonalignment and African socialism. It is a sad mistake to think that you can get more food, more hospitals or schools by crying 'Communism.' There is no room here for the lazy or idle. There is no room for those who wait for things to be given for nothing. There is no place for leaders to build a nation on slogans!"

The West was impressed by Kenyatta's firmness in rejecting a Communist solution to Kenya's problems, but wished he would get rid of Odinga the way he had dumped Kaggia.

Kenyatta, however, was shrewdly aware that Odinga as Vice-President under his control was safer than Odinga out of the government. As leader of the Luo, he would be certain to try to bring down the republic by uniting the forces of tribalism and communism.

Kenyatta's method of coping with Odinga was more adroit. He managed to reduce Odinga's supply of Chinese and Russian funds, and spike efforts by Odinga and Kaggia to woo tribal leaders.

One day police informed him that a convoy of Chinese arms was passing through Odinga's electoral district, and that a large cache was being stored in the basement of Odinga's office. Kenyatta immediately ordered the commander of the British armed forces to seize the weapons.

Learning that someone, probably Odinga, had also ordered an official shipment of Russian arms, Kenyatta rejected the shipment as "obsolete." To warn Odinga, he bluntly expelled several Communist diplomats and journalists who were close friends of the Vice-President. At cabinet meetings he began to ignore Odinga pointedly, conferring principally with Mboya and other ministers who favored the West.

Visibly upset by this open rebuff, Odinga could scarcely steel himself to show up for cabinet meetings. A foreign correspondent asked him about his Communist ties.

"Communism is food to me," Odinga replied defiantly.

Kenyatta retaliated by removing him from the leadership of the Kenya delegation bound for the annual Commonwealth Conference in London. Their clash was now an open one.

Understandably pleased, both Washington and London began viewing the tough old *Mzee* as a "dependable" African leader whose shrewd decisions were based on common sense and mature judgment. Sir Malcolm MacDonald, the last British governor of Kenya, summed up Western opinion by describing Kenyatta affectionately as "a wise old owl."

"Once they called me a Red-winged blackbird," he chuckled at a cabinet meeting, "and turned me into a jailbird!"

He knew that the real answer to communism was not suppression but providing jobs for his people. KANU's crash educational program was turning out increasing thousands of high school and college graduates every year. Yet in almost three years of independence, only 130,000 jobs in industry and commerce had been found for black Kenyans.

The Luo held most of the good city jobs that had been opened to Africans during the emergency, while 80,000 Kikuyu had been held in restriction on the reserves. Now two million Kikuyu were resentful. Why did *Mzee,* a Kikuyu himself, permit this injustice to continue?

Nairobi was crowded with an influx of ragged and homeless youth who often went hungry for days at a time. Calling themselves Young Wingers, they picketed KANU headquarters and broke into government offices to demand either jobs or handouts. At one cabinet meeting a minister pointed out the window to a group of them sitting around idly.

"Some live on grass," he said. "What can we do?"

"The only thing we *can* do," Kenyatta decided apprehensively. "Africanize more jobs—in a hurry."

More and more white and Asian employees in the banks, shops, customs, post office and elsewhere began to find themselves replaced by Africans. Kenyatta selected the leading hotel in Mombasa, Kenya's chief seaport, for a key experiment. He replaced the hotel's British receptionists, Asian cashiers, Italian headwaiters and bartenders with an all-African staff. Could total "Africanization" work?

The result was an immediate, serious deterioration in the hotel's services. Outraged tourists and business visitors complained bitterly. The inexperienced natives were overwhelmed by the sophisticated expectations of the guests.

Kenyatta was deeply worried. It was obvious that he would have to move slowly in transferring non-African jobs into the hands of his people. The economy might collapse under the burden of ineptitude resulting from unskilled workers in skilled jobs. Yet how could he expect his poor starving people to understand the need for delay?

Another important consideration led him to slow down his Africanization policy. The white and Asian populations were growing increasingly skeptical of his promise that Kenya would operate as a "multiracial society." If they felt that their future was in jeopardy, there might be a mass exodus, causing economic paralysis.

Brooding over the problem, Kenyatta decided he had to provide a new direction and goal for Kenya's youth. On September 11, 1964, he appeared on Kenya's new television network to address the nation. Young men were mistaken, he warned, to believe that the way to get ahead was to leave the villages to look for jobs in the cities.

"They leave their land unattended, or in the care of old mothers, wives or young brothers . . . and spend many months living on relatives and friends, and being generally a nuisance," he deplored. "Such people distort the purchasing power of their relatives and friends, making them poorer and miserable, and also interfere with the social plans and provisions for the genuine residents of the towns."

Deploring the sponger as "a disgrace to his manhood and to our society," he urged city dwellers to send such parasites home. "Whereas we believe in African socialism," he declared, "we do not believe in loitering and laziness. We believe in cooperatives, but not in promoting a state of affairs in which some people try to live on the sweat of others." He eulogized farming as the best way of life for most Kenyans: "Try to serve your country and to farm well, because all good things come from the soil."

His new slogan was: "Out of the Cities—Back to the Land!" Tom Mboya was given the job of making it do for Kenya what Horace Greeley's famous cry, "Go West, Young Man, Go West," had done for Americans in opening up their land.

Both Odinga and Kaggia challenged Kenyatta's sincerity. If he *really* wanted to resettle the jobless on the land, why didn't he seize all white settlers' farms in the Highlands and divide them up among African smallholders?

Mboya issued a policy paper pointing out that there was already a shortage of corn. A breakup of the remaining big European farms could mean famine. Besides, Mboya argued, what was the good of substituting a black class of country squires for white? "No class problem exists today among Africans," he wrote proudly, and the only way to prevent one was through large-scale farming by African cooperatives.

He planned to persuade Great Britain to lend Kenya the necessary millions to implement the development of cooperatives in tribal areas where such farms were most needed.

Kaggia promptly charged that Mboya's policy paper had been drawn up for him by "imperialist experts" among his advisers, to protect the British white settlers from having their Highlands farms confiscated. Other criticism came from the Young Wingers, who claimed that the government was ducking the real issue—jobs in the cities. They made it plain that the prospect of farm life frankly bored them.

Kenyatta, who had a religious reverence for the soil, was shocked. Every morning he spent hours working on his home farm before leaving for his office. It deeply depressed him that thousands of Kenya's youth had so little interest in the land—the land for which so many of their parents had given their lives in the struggle for independence, for which he had sacrificed nine years in desert prisons.

Oginga Odinga now felt that the fresh winds of change were blowing from the East. The time had come to challenge the aging lion of Kenya, who had ruled the pride too long. Ignored and isolated in the cabinet, Odinga moreover saw no point in continuing to let Kenyatta keep him in political handcuffs. Moving swiftly, he hurled a thunderbolt.

He resigned as Vice-President. Withdrawing from KANU, he led twenty-eight members of Parliament and two assistant ministers into a new party of opposition— the Kenya People's Union (KPU). Ignoring the well-known fact that he had accepted hundreds of thousands of dollars from both Peking and Moscow, he charged that Kenya had been taken over by an "invisible government" representing Western interests.

In a bold speech to Parliament, Odinga acknowledged that he intended to topple the Kenyatta government. "Today we have come out in our full colors," he shouted defiantly.

Kenyatta's Minister for Information, Achieng Oneko, also defected to the new KPU. Oneko was a Luo tribesman who, like Kenyatta, had spent many years in British prisons. He accused Kenyatta of failing to keep his election promises, and threw a bombshell at other

KANU leaders. "Personal gain," he charged, "has become the guiding star in the party."

His chief target was Tom Mboya, who owned a hundred well-tailored suits, drove a Mercedes, and lived in a predominantly white suburb of Nairobi with his attractive, well-dressed and American-educated wife, Pamela. Other cabinet ministers, it could not be denied, also lived extremely well.

The tribal conflict Kenyatta had tried so long to avoid—Kikuyu versus Luo—was reflected in KANU versus Odinga's KPU. Some Luo were now pressing Odinga to split Nyanza Province from the republic as the "United Kingdom of Kisumu" under His Majesty Oginga Odinga. Faced with secession and civil war, wrathful seventy-six-year-old Jomo Kenyatta rose to the challenge.

Calling a press conference at State House, he blistered the defection of Odinga and his supporters as "a kind of emotional spasm" without any real significance. "Their following is negligible," he declared contemptuously. "Their power is nil." Then the old lion of Kikuyu bared his teeth.

"I intend to recall Parliament to pass legislation that will compel Odinga and his followers to resign their seats in Parliament and seek reelection from their districts," he announced with obvious relish. "They must go back to the voters and state their case against my government!"

To Odinga's dismay, Kenyatta called Parliament into emergency session. With a clear majority in the 130-member House of Representatives, he had no difficulty in winning a constitutional amendment forcing all KPU members to resign and stand for reelection against KANU.

Infuriated, Odinga sought out a group of ex-Mau Mau leaders and offered to recruit a new forest army for them if they agreed to fight Kenyatta as they had once fought the colonial government. Some Mau Mau were tempted by Odinga's offer to finance them to the extent of almost half a million dollars, but others were outraged by his treason.

Informed of the plot, Kenyatta swiftly called a giant mass rally in Nairobi, where four ex-guerrilla leaders told the story to a shocked crowd. Thousands of Kikuyu roared their rage at Odinga and the KPU. *Mzee* growled a public warning at his former Vice-President: "If you play around with me, Odinga, you'll be playing around with a lion!"

Half of the members of Parliament who had left KANU to join KPU abruptly changed their minds. In a last speech before leaving Parliament, Odinga accused Kenyatta of unfair tactics, and of planning to spend government funds to defeat KPU in the coming elections. "But it doesn't matter what the government does," he cried angrily. "Despite this intimidation, we are going to exist as an opposition!"

The nation waited breathlessly for the outcome of the first real challenge to the power of Jomo Kenyatta.

Would the flag flying over Kenya soon turn Red?

15 ‹‹‹‹‹‹‹‹‹‹‹‹‹‹‹‹‹‹

Kenyatta's Country, Today and Tomorrow

PREPARING FOR THE NEW ELECTIONS, KENYATTA RE-shuffled his cabinet. With one exception all his ministers were now pro-West moderates. The exception was his replacement for Odinga as Vice-President—Foreign Minister Joseph Murumbi. A leftist, Murumbi frequently made anti-Western statements that irked Kenyatta. But he was nevertheless loyal to the republic, Kenyatta knew, and useful to keep the West guessing.

The foreign embassies in Kenya watched for a clue to a shift in foreign policy in Murumbi's replacement as Foreign Minister. *Mzee* had a surprise for them. "The new Foreign Minister," he revealed with a smile, "will be Jomo Kenyatta. Only in this way will both the East and West understand the simple truth that Kenya stands only for Kenya, and for the struggle of all African peoples toward fredom!"

A three-week political campaign between KANU and KPU created great national excitement. Odinga toured the countryside in his black Mercedes, wooing voters with promises of free land, free education, jobs for everyone.

"The country is under the thumb of Europeans!"

he shouted to crowds. "Kenyatta is told what to do by the Americans. The whites should all be kicked out."

He charged that if KPU failed to win all available seats, it would only prove that the elections were rigged. He attacked Kenyatta personally as both a dictatorial tyrant and a coward who feared opposition. "You can be a friend of Kenyatta's," he accused, "only if you crawl and cringe like a hyena. He is a frightened man with a small heart."

KANU's campaign used wit and derision against the KPU. Africans had a superstitious dread of the *kipu* (chameleon), so KPU was branded the "chameleon party" that had changed color from black, red and green —the national flag colors of the republic—to bright red.

Speaking at a huge Nairobi rally, Kenyatta reserved his greatest wrath for his onetime fellow prisoner, Bildad Kaggia. He could privately understand the defection of Odinga, as leader of the Luo. But he could not forgive Kaggia—the only Kikuyu in the leadership of the KPU—for what he considered base disloyalty. Kaggia, *Mzee* charged furiously, was a captive of the Communists, a liar, a cheat.

He accused Odinga of trying to buy votes. "If these people offer money," he warned his listeners, "you must know it is foreign money meant to undermine the sovereignty of our country. Beware of this political prostitution." The rally rocked with laughter as he added with a wry grin, "But take the money—and *then* vote for KANU!"

Although he scorned buying votes for KANU, Kenyatta was not above offering traditional blandishments. Most of the electorate went to the polls in high spirits thanks to gourds of African beer doled out by KANU campaigners.

The world press followed the election of May, 1966 closely, aware that an Odinga victory would upset the balance of power in east Africa.

The lion of Kenya waited tensely for the results of the election to tell him whether he still had the confidence of his people, or whether his life's work was over.

When the returns were counted, they indicated a landslide victory for Jomo Kenyatta. KANU increased its plurality in the House to 121 against KPU's 7, in the Senate to 39 against KPU's 2. Kaggia had even lost his own bid for a seat by a sweeping margin of 18,000 votes. The political futures of Kaggia and Odinga were bankrupt.

Studying the election results, Kenyatta found that the antiwhite racist appeals of Odinga and Kaggia had met their greatest response in Luo country, but had fallen flat in the cities. Africans in the cities, he surmised, recognized the importance of the white community in keeping the economy afloat. Kenyatta determined to pursue even more vigorously his policy of accommodation with Kenya's whites.

When one white government employee complained to him of being radically insulted by an African member of Parliament, Kenyatta immediately phoned the MP. "You will now go to the office of the European and apologize," he ordered wrathfully. "If you do not apologize, you are *out!*"

His multiracial policy came under attack from an unexpected source. In November, 1967, America's black power advocate, Stokely Carmichael, visited Africa, vowing, "Africa is our motherland!" But finding only a cool reception for his antiwhite credo, he attacked Kenyatta and other leaders of former British colonies in Africa as "traitors and clowns." Their multiracialism, he charged, was just "nonsensical talk . . . a trick by the white man to keep Africa divided."

Disdaining to reply, Kenyatta let the African National Congress speak for him. This revolutionary group, opposed to racist South Africa, dismissed Carmichael as a demagogue: "His stream of coarse invective . . . and naïve manner dismayed and mystified all those who have the interest of African aspirations at heart."

In contrast, *Mzee* was grieved by the assassination of another American black leader he greatly respected—Martin Luther King.

One of Kenyatta's most serious problems stemmed from the demands of his ministers that he proceed with Africanization at the expense of Kenya's East Indian population. He resisted this pressure as weakening his multiracial policy. But he knew there was a great deal of bitter feeling toward Indian merchants for taking advantage of Africans, cheating them as customers and exploiting them as employees.

Many black Kenyans also resented the Indians for being as color-prejudiced against them as the Europeans. And from a coldly practical standpoint, the Indians were not as essential to Kenya's economy as the Europeans. Most Asians, understandably nervous now about their status, scrutinized every statement by Kenyatta with apprehensive sensitivity.

As early as June, 1964, Kenyatta had warned Indian businessmen in Nairobi, that, while he hoped to retain their skills and business experience, they would have to adapt themselves to live with Africans and "obey the African rule."

He had sounded an ominous note: "I say that if there are any Asians who are unwilling to work with us, they can pack their bags and go." Early in 1968, still unable to solve his major problem of unemployment, he yielded to the pressure of his ministers to Africanize the jobs and property controlled by Kenya's 167,000 Indians. Parliament began passing anti-Indian legislation. Panic swept the Asian population. Those who had prudently obtained British passports sold out their businesses for whatever they could get.

They flew off to London's Heathrow airport at the rate of 700 a day. Long lines formed before the British consulate in Nairobi as thousands of frantic Indians belatedly sought passports. The alarmed Labor government of England, worried about floods of Asian immigrants for whom there were no homes, jobs or welfare services, quickly rammed a new restrictive immigration law through Commons. Excluded were those whose parents or grandparents had not been born in Britain, except for a token annual quota of 1,500.

Kenyatta's hard-line policy toward the East Indians had the effect of a shock wave on the British Commonwealth. Member countries were stunned by the realization that no longer could any citizen of the Commonwealth travel freely from one sister nation to another. Worse, Britain's new law implied that one Commonwealth nation's racial strain was now considered less desirable than another's.

Still worse, Kenyatta had forced England to repudiate the promise by former Foreign Secretary Duncan Sandys that after Kenya became a republic, "all foreign settlers" who preferred English to Kenyan citizenship would be given British passports. Stormy clashes broke out in England between citizens who insisted that the government must keep faith with Kenya's East Indians and labor union members who wanted them barred from Britain as Asian job competition.

The British government appealed to Kenyatta to

ease his pressures on the Indians. Agreeing, he tried to reassure them, but the frightened Asians neither believed nor trusted him. They were convinced that however fair Kenyatta himself might try to be, the intensity of anti-Indian feeling in Kenya's Parliament would force him to discriminate against them. At the time this book is being written, most Indians would leave Kenya if Britain agreed to take them in.

The unique leadership of Jomo Kenyatta has brought the Republic of Kenya a long way in the short time since *Uhuru,* but there is an even longer way to go before all his dreams for his people can be realized.

Manufacturing has increased steadily, thanks to new investments attracted to Kenya by foreign confidence in the stability of Kenyatta's regime. Export markets are guaranteed not only by the United Kingdom and the United States, but also by the East African Common Market, which unites Uganda and Tanzania with industrialized Kenya.

Kenya's $13.4 million of exports to the United States are chiefly pyrethrum (for insecticides), wattle extract (gum arabic for perfumes, medicine, candy, mucilage), sisal (for rope), coffee, hides and skins. These exports are paid for by United States imports—chiefly machinery, cars and petroleum products.

No one recognizes better than Kenyatta himself that the prosperity of his country still depends largely on European entrepreneurship. Very little of Kenya's major manufacturing, trade or commerce is yet in African hands.

Kenyatta's Minister for Agriculture is a white South African, and the top-ranking officer in the Kenya Army is an Englishman. The Commissioner of Police is an African, but his deputy is a white man. Until Africans can be trained to replace them, 1,500 white men hold important jobs in the Kenya civil service, their salaries paid by the British.

Some Africans are now on the boards of directors of Kenya's big companies, and others have titled positions without responsibility. But otherwise almost all the top jobs in the business world are still manned by white men.

The changeover of much farmland from British to African hands, however, has created serious problems. The less efficient farming methods of most unskilled Africans sent the yield of coffee, tea, pyrethrum, sisal and other farm products plummeting to a disastrously low level. Kenya's farm revenues were also worsened by drought and a drop in prices on the world market. Today only 900 white plantations remain, waiting for the government to buy them out.

Kenyatta hopes that, with experience, the agricultural picture will brighten. Meanwhile, always seeking new sources of wealth for the country, he is cultivating the booming tourist trade. From 1965 to 1967 the number of tourists attracted to Kenya's tropical beauty and game reserves from America and Europe jumped from 74,000 to over 135,000.

Nairobi today is a gleaming, modern capital of baby skyscrapers, tall hotels and traffic jams unsnarled with cool efficiency by smartly clad African policemen. Tourists, ignoring an underbrush of crowded little Indian shops and African tin-roofed shacks, spend a typical three days in Nairobi strolling broad avenues made brilliant with scarlet bougainvillea and sipping cocktails at sidewalk cafés.

Then they trek into the bush with guides to explore the game parks with cameras, or climb up Mount Kenya to the snowline riding "zebronkeys" (crossed zebras and donkeys). Rich sportsmen pay $12,000 a month to hunt elephant, lion, leopard, rhino and buffalo with some of the world's top hunters.

So fast is Kenya booming as a tourist mecca that British and American airlines are both scrambling to build luxurious new hotels in Nairobi and Mombasa.

Shrewdly aware of the value of publicity to Kenya tourism, Kenyatta acts as official starter for Kenya's East African Safari Rally, the world's most grueling international auto race. In 1968, when 92 African and foreign cars competed in the 3,000-mile course, only seven drivers were left in the race after four days. The winner was a Kenyan, continuing an unbroken string of African victories. "We would all be pleased if an overseas driver were to win," *Mzee* observed. "Provided, of course, it did not become a habit!" He was also delighted when eight Kenyans won medals at the Mexican Olympics.

Perhaps the biggest worry of seventy-eight-year-old Jomo Kenyatta today is the continued exodus of those white farmers and civil servants he still needs. On what used to be the White Highlands, many farmhouses stand vacant, their fields untended. More and more offices fall empty in Nairobi as businesses that depended on the white farmers dwindle.

Of the original 67,000 whites in Kenya before independence, only half remain. Living side by side with Kenyatta's people, they send their children to integrated schools and mix socially with Africans.

As for the grizzled old lion of Kenya himself, he avoids social contacts, living simply close to the soil. His new farmhouse at Ichaweri, his birthplace thirty miles north of Nairobi, looks out toward the view that has had deep significance for him all of his life—the snow-crowned peak of Kere-Nyaga, home of the god Nagai.

Seeing no close friends outside of his immediate

family, he bestows all his affection and free time on his shy fourth wife, Ngina, and their four children. He has not forsaken his other wives, keeping in close touch with all three families, including his white wife Edna and son Peter in England. Vague about the exact number of all his children, he indicated in 1968 that the oldest, a son, was then fifty.

An ardent gardener, he rises at 6:00 A.M. each morning to visit his farm while an aide accompanies him, briefing him on the day's official agenda.

At 8:15 his aides and five bodyguards begin the daily thirty-mile trip by car to Nairobi, where he works a nine-to-four day in a modest office in the seven-story Ministry of Public Works building. Bored by administrative details at this late time of life, he refuses to read memos or documents, demanding that his ministers render verbal accounts of their activities. There are whispers of another reason: failing eyesight.

He gets home before 5:00 P.M., unless there is a crisis to keep him longer. Tossing aside his famous beaded cap, double-breasted lounge suit and treasured London School of Economics tie, he wanders around his farmyard in an old orange shirt, gray slacks and sandals with the word *Uhuru* burned into the leather. Afterward he will lie down on a worn, blue leather couch in his 1,000-book library to read books on gardening, or favorite passages in Shakespeare, the Bible and the Koran and other Oriental religious works.

Looking back over his long and incredible life, Jomo Kenyatta has much to be proud of. Jailed and persecuted as a dangerous firebrand, he has changed the world's image of him to that of a great African statesman, an example of stability, reasonableness and skillful leadership. He has largely ended tribal and racial strife in

Kenya. He has proved a shield, not a sword, for the whites who had feared him.

"We used to hate Kenyatta's guts," said one white farmer in Nakuru. "Now he's probably the best chance we've got. Besides, we hate to think of what will come after him."

"I am fairly optimistic that he means what he says about cooperation with the whites," said one former high-ranking British official. "But the thing I worry about is if he can't make a go of it economically, if he doesn't get the proper finance, if the Somali erupt, if tribal discontent explodes, then he might well look around for a scapegoat and blame the white man."

Alex Ward, Director of Kenya National Farmers' Union, said grimly, "Looking at it over a longish period, I would say that eventually most white farmers in Kenya will be gone."

But to the Africans of Kenya, *Mzee* is the George Washington of his country. The superstitious revere him as a god who will join the other gods on Mount Kenya. The educated see him as the enigmatic personification of Africa itself, with all its conflicts, contradictions and mystery. But for both he is the African leader who best symbolizes their struggle for independence, learning and personal dignity.

As for the world, it cannot help but admire the remarkable qualities of an African shepherd boy, son of a tribal farmer, grandson of a rainmaking magician, who rose to become the sophisticated leader of his nation and an important influence in the shaping of a new Africa.

Whether all that he has built will be swept away with his death is an open question. Western leaders are apprehensive because today it is the enormous prestige of only one man who keeps Kenya united—a man soon to be eighty. Perhaps the hope for the Kenya of tomorrow

184

will lie in the corps of young Africans he has sent to study at the universities of America, England and the Soviet Union.

Meanwhile, the story of Kenyatta is fraught with significance for an America today faced with the demands of twenty million of its black citizens for social justice.

The United States stands at the crossroads of race war and *Harambee*. Must we reap the whirlwind with an American version of Mau Mau? Or will we follow the teachings of Martin Luther King and the mature Jomo Kenyatta, to work together in peace to build a new, better multiracial society?

Suggested Further Reading

Bennett, George. *Kenya: A Political History*. London, Ibadan, Nairobi, Accra: Oxford University Press, 1963.

Bennett, George, and Carl G. Rosberg. *The Kenyatta Election*. London, New York, Nairobi: Oxford University Press, 1961.

Burnett, Hugh (ed.). *Face to Face*. New York: Stein and Day, Publishers, 1965.

Cohen, John. *Africa Addio*. New York: Ballantine Books, 1966.

Cox, Richard. *Kenyatta's Country*. New York, Washington: Frederick A. Praeger Publishers, 1965.

Kenyatta, Jomo. *Facing Mount Kenya*. New York: Vintage Books, undated.

Kenyatta, Jomo. *Harambee!* Nairobi, London, New York: Oxford University Press, 1964.

Mboya, Tom. *Freedom and After*. Nairobi: Government Printer, 1965.

Slater, Montague. *The Trial of Jomo Kenyatta*. London: Secker & Warburg, 1955.

Articles and news stories on Jomo Kenyatta consulted for this book were found in *Commonweal, Harper's, Life, Nation, New Republic, Newsweek, New York Times Magazine, Readers Digest, Reporter, Time* and *U.S. News and World Report.*

Index

Aberdare Mts., 111, 157
Abrahams, Peter, 52, 60
Africa, 26, 60, 62, 105, 108, 116, 143, 146, 153, 160, 161, 165, 175, 177, 178
African Land Settlement & Utilization Board, 69
African National Conf., 178
Africanization, 152, 168, 169, 178, 179
Age Groups, 17, 18, 32-34
Agitation, 41-44, 46, 47, 52, 53, 56, 57, 64, 65, 69, 70, 75, 80, 83-85, 96-98
Angola, 146
Anthropology, 55-57
Army revolt, 151, 152
Atrocities, 74, 75, 77, 82, 86, 87, 89, 91, 92, 99-101, 103, 109-112, 157

Back-to-the-land movement, 169-171
Baluhya tribe, 11, 121
Bantu tribe, 12, 25, 29
Baring, Sir Evelyn, 88, 89, 92, 100, 112, 115
Bible, 31, 32, 43, 95, 183
Black Nationalism, 7, 8, 60, 177
Bowyer, Eric, 91
British Commissioners, 23, 24, 26, 33, 44, 58, 68, 69, 72, 81, 88, 92, 101, 103, 104, 112, 115-118, 121-125, 128, 129, 131, 132, 167
British East Africa Co., 23

British Governors, *see* British Commissioners
British Labor Party, 58, 80, 93, 95, 112, 115, 179
British White Papers, 43, 49, 50, 118
Brockway, Fenner, 93

Cabinet, 134, 167, 168, 171, 172, 175
Carmichael, Stokley, 177, 178
Carter Kenya Land Comm., 51, 52
Caste system, 33, 40, 108, 170
Central Province, 86
China, 153, 167
Chou En-lai, 153
Christianity, 29, 31, 45, 76, 84, 96, 98, 107
Church of Scotland, 28, 29, 31, 44, 45, 48, 49, 51
Churchill, Winston, 34
Civil War, 89, 90, 99-101, 104, 110, 111, 116
Clark, Edna Grace, 57
Cold War, 142, 149, 159, 161, 164
Colonialism, *see* Imperialism
Colonists' Assn., 33, 37
Colonization, 22-27
Coming-of-age rites, 32, 44, 49, 73
Commonwealth Conferences, 159, 167
Communism, 9, 47, 50, 52, 53, 57, 85, 86, 95, 127, 133, 134,

142, 147, 164-168, 173, 176
Congo, 134, 148, 149, 163-165
Corfield Report, 118, 127
Corruption, 79, 93, 140, 155-157, 172, 176, 178
Crown Land Ordinance, 36, 38, 39, 46, 97, 154

Delamere, Lord, 148
Dini ya Jesu Kristo Sect, 51, 73, 76
Discrimination, 40, 48, 49, 54, 59, 60, 63, 96, 98, 108, 130, 165, 185
Dulles, John Foster, 142, 143

East Africa, 34
East Indians, 23, 24, 33, 37, 39, 47, 48, 61, 85, 108, 120, 127, 134, 148, 149, 168, 169, 178-180
Eisenhower administration, 142
Egypt, 135, 159
Elections, 117, 119-123, 127, 133, 172, 173, 175-177
Eliot, Sir Charles, 26, 27
Elizabeth, Queen, 86
Embu tribe, 84
Emergency Proclamations, 88, 89, 118, 144
England, see Great Britain
European travels, 50, 51, 53, 56, 59, 61

Facing Mt. Kenya, 56, 57, 80
Family, 11-16, 28, 49
Fanon, Dr. Frantz, 8, 9
Fed. of East Africa, 154, 180
Forced labor, 33, 34, 37, 39, 42, 44, 46, 79, 97, 113
Foreign Aid, 147, 159-161, 170
Fort Dagoretti, 23, 24
Fort Hall, 28, 34, 44, 71, 77, 122
Forty Group, the, 73-75, 82, 87-89
Freeman, John, 32

Gatunda, 100
Germany, 50, 57, 64
Ghana, 52, 116, 118, 135
Gichuru, James, 58, 59, 70, 119-122, 125, 131, 134, 159
Githunguri, 45, 68-70, 75
Great Britain, 23, 24, 51, 52, 59, 64, 67, 80, 107, 108, 110-112, 119, 135, 142, 143, 146, 149-151, 159-161, 164, 170, 179-181, 185
Grievances, native, 33, 34, 36, 37, 39, 41, 44, 46, 47, 59, 62, 63, 71-73, 76, 86, 98, 104
Grogan, Lt. Col. Ewart Scott, 26, 27, 33, 34, 37, 39

Hale, Little, 93
Harambee, 136, 140, 141, 144, 149, 156, 163, 164, 185
Hilton Young Royal Comm., 47
House of Commons, London, 49

Ichaweri, 11, 13, 14, 21, 27, 34, 36, 39, 40, 47, 67, 88, 112, 182
Imperialism, 26, 146, 160, 166
Imprisonment, 41, 47, 68, 88-129
Independence Day, 142-148, 165
Independence movement, 46, 57, 65, 76, 79-81, 96, 112, 113, 116, 117, 123, 125, 127, 128, 131, 136, 137
Indians, see East Indians
Integration, 80, 127, 130, 140, 141, 169, 177, 178, 180-182, 184, 185
Int. Institute of African Languages & Culture, 55
Int. Negro Workers' Congress, 50

Job training, 34, 37, 38, 154, 168, 169, 180, 181
Johnson, Lyndon B., 159

Kaggia, Bildad, 93, 158, 159, 165-167, 170, 176, 177

Kamau wa Ngengi, *see* Kenyatta, Jomo
Kamba tribe, 12, 22, 44, 120, 149
Kangethe, Joseph, 47, 75
Kapenguria, 93, 94, 99, 101
Kapila, A. P., 108
Kariuki, Jesse, 75
kebata celebrations, 14
Kemathi, Dedan, 148
Kennedy, John F., 142, 143
Kenya African Dem. Union (KADU), 121-123, 125, 128, 129, 132, 133, 136, 149, 163, 164
Kenya African Nat. Union (KANU), 120-125, 128, 129, 131-133, 149, 152, 153, 163, 165, 168, 171-173, 176, 177
Kenya African Study Union (KASU), 58-60
Kenya African Union (KAU), 60, 62, 63, 65, 67, 68, 70-72, 75, 76, 80-83, 85, 88, 89, 93, 94, 96, 98, 104, 105, 107, 108, 111, 119, 131
Kenya Citizens' Assoc., 80, 81
Kenya: Land of Conflict, 59
Kenya Legislature, 119, 127, 133, 135, 143, 149, 152, 159, 161, 163, 171-173, 177, 179, 180
Kenya Nat. Farmers' Union, 184
Kenya Nat. Police Air Wing, 160
Kenya People's Union (KPU), 171-173, 176, 177
Kenya Rifles, 146, 149, 151, 180
Kenya Supreme Court, 38, 39, 94, 95, 107, 108
Kenya Teachers' College, 68-70, 72
kenyatta, 39, 40, 44, 155
Kenyatta, Edna (wife), 58, 60, 61, 165, 183
Kenyatta, Jomo (Kamau wa Ngengi), significance, 7-10; born in Kikuyu tribe, 11; childhood, 12-17; grandfather's influence, 18-21; learns Kenya history, 22-27; educated at Mission, 28-34; undergoes age-group ceremony, and marries, 32-36; fights Crown Land Ordinance, 37-39; turns agitator, 39-47; goes to Europe, 48-54; writes *"Facing Mt. Kenya,"* 55-57; third marriage, and the war years, 58-61; post-war return to Kenya, 61-68; wins control of native schools and KAU, 67-73; ambiguous relations with Mau Mau, 73-87; arrested, 88, 89; trial, 91-105; imprisonment, 105-129; campaigns for independence, 129-132; elected Prime Minister, 133-138; appeals to white settlers for cooperation, 139-141; achieves independence for Kenya, 142-148; faces problems of new nation, 149-162; defeats Communist challenge, 163-177; Africanizes jobs of East Indians, 178-180; recent years, 180-185
Kenyatta, Ngina (wife), 67, 125, 129, 183
Kenyatta, Peter (son), 58, 60, 61, 165, 183
Kerner Comm., 9
Kiambu, 83, 97, 99, 125
Kikuyu African Orth. Church, 45
Kikuyu Assoc., 41
Kikuyu Central Assoc. (KCA), 44-47, 53, 54, 56-58, 63, 68, 74-76, 94, 96, 98, 144, 155
Kikuyu customs, 10-21, 25-27, 29-32, 34-39, 44, 55, 56, 62, 71, 77
Kikuyu Ind. Pentecostal Church, 45
Kikuyu Ind. Schools Assoc. (KISA), 45, 46, 69, 70, 81, 82
Kikuyu Maranga African Union (KMAU), 74

Kikuyu people, 10-12, 22, 100, 101, 103, 109-111, 116, 117, 120, 122, 129, 135, 136, 149, 166, 168, 173
King, Martin Luther, 7, 9, 178, 185
King's African Rifles, 26, 38, 62, 64, 73, 89, 110, 149
Kioi, Chief, 38, 39
Kipsigis tribe, 91, 92, 100, 101, 103, 121, 144
Kitale, 94
Koinange, Mbui, 53, 56, 58, 59, 68, 69, 81
Kongo wa Magana (grandfather), 18, 19, 21, 22, 47, 155

Lancashire Fusiliers, 88, 89
Land Freedom Army, 89, 103, 104, 110, 111, 116, 144
Land resettlement, 120, 132, 144, 145, 154, 156, 158
Land sales, 17, 25, 36, 38
Lanet Camp, 151
Lari, 101
League Against Imperialism, 50
Leakey, Dr. L. S. B., 94
Lecturing, 57
Legislative Council, 33, 34, 36, 41, 42, 44, 47, 59, 68, 73, 76, 80, 85, 87, 92, 96, 107, 108, 112, 117-119, 123, 131
Lenin School, 53
Lodwar, 109, 118, 121, 123, 124
Lokitaung, 105, 108, 118
London, 47, 48, 50-52, 59, 61, 119, 120, 150, 159, 164, 165, 167
London Colonial Office, 32, 33, 36, 43, 47-52, 75, 80, 93, 119, 120
London Communist Party, 53
London Privy Council, 108, 112
London School of Econ. & Political Science, 55, 183
Luka, Chief, 101

Lumumba Institute, 165, 166
Luo tribe, 12, 117, 118, 120, 121, 133, 143, 149, 166, 168, 171, 172, 176, 177
Lyttelton, Oliver, 93

McCarthy, Sen. Joseph, 175
MacDonald, Gov. Sir Malcolm, 146, 167
Macleod, Ian, 119
Malinowski, Bronislaw, 55, 56
Maralal, 124, 125, 127-129
Marriages, 35, 36, 40, 58, 67, 165, 183
Marshall, Thurgood, 119
Masai tribe, 15, 18, 22, 121, 122, 143
Masters' & Servants' Ordinance, 33
Mathu, Eliud, 59
Mau Mau, 7, 8, 26, 72-105, 123, 124, 137, 141, 144, 145, 147, 148, 157-160, 165, 173, 185
Mbotela, Tom, 80, 81
Mboya, Tom, 115-117, 119-123, 125, 132-134, 136, 162, 167, 170, 172
Meiklejohn, E., 91, 92
Meinertzhagen, Capt., 26, 72, 73
Meru tribe, 44, 79, 84
Mikongoe tree, 83, 97
Missionaries, 27-32, 34, 36, 37, 44, 45, 55, 62
Mitchell, Sir Philip, 68, 69, 72, 73, 84
Mogo, 21, 22
Moigai (brother), 11, 13
Mombasa, 22-24, 33, 48, 61, 62, 64, 72, 115, 136, 168, 182
moramati (trustees), 17, 25, 38
Mortimer, Sir Charles, 81, 82
Moscow, 50, 53, 86, 95, 133, 146, 165, 166, 171
Mount Kenya (Kere-Nyaga), 11, 22, 27, 31, 34, 70, 73, 74, 108, 111, 124, 181, 182, 184

Mount Kilimanjaro, 144
Mozambique, 146
Muigwithania, 46
Murumbi, Joseph, 175
My People of Kenya, 57

Nairobi, 11, 24, 27, 33, 39-41,
  44, 47, 50, 51, 61, 62, 64, 73,
  82, 86-89, 92, 93, 101, 108,
  111, 122, 124, 129, 135, 142,
  143, 148, 149, 153, 158, 160,
  161, 166, 168, 172, 173, 176,
  178, 179, 181-183
Nakuru Town Hall, 140, 141,
  184
Nandi tribe, 23, 121
Nationalization, 153, 154, 157,
  158, 170
Native Authority Ordinance, 46
Natives, pro-British, 43, 148
Neutrality, 159, 160, 164, 165,
  175, 177
Ngai (god), 11, 22, 27, 31, 34,
  74, 95, 108, 182
Ngala, Ronald, 128, 129, 131,
  132, 163
Ngei, Paul, 123
Ngengi (father), 11, 12, 14-17,
  28, 35, 47
Nkrumah, Kwame, 52, 60, 118
Northern Province, 41, 105, 149,
  152
Nyanza Province, 118, 172
Nyerere, Julius, 151
Nyeri, 36

Oaths, secret, 14, 32, 43, 74-77,
  80-82, 84, 85, 88, 89, 95, 123,
  157, 158
Odede, F. W., 107
Odinga, Jaromogi "Oginga," 118,
  120-123, 125, 132-134, 153,
  154, 160, 162, 165, 166, 167,
  170-173, 175, 176, 177
Oneko, Achieng, 171
Operation Anvil, 111, 116

Organization of African Unity
  (OAU), 152

Pan-African Union Movement,
  52, 60
Parliament (British), 49, 93, 95,
  116, 179
Peking, 133, 166, 171
Political Reforms, 81, 82, 87, 96,
  99, 117-120, 132, 163
Polygamy, 31, 32, 96
Presidency, 146
Prince Philip, 145
Pritt, Denis N., 94, 95, 99, 107,
  108
Products, 180, 181

Racism, 135, 141, 143, 153, 165,
  177-180, 185
Railroad, 23, 24
Rebellion, 54, 59, 63, 68, 72, 80,
  81, 84, 86-89, 104, 110, 161,
  173
Renison, Sir Patrick, 121, 123-
  125, 127-129, 131, 132, 141
Republic of Kenya, 10, 138, 139,
  142, 145, 153, 156, 160, 165,
  180
Reserves, native, 36, 37, 43, 58,
  62, 63, 76, 77, 79, 100, 108,
  112, 168
Rift Valley, 63, 108, 124, 158
Robeson, Paul, 52
Ruark, Robert, 85, 95
Ruck, Roger, 101
Ruiru River, 82

Samburu tribe, 144
Sanders of the River, 52
Sartre, Jean-Paul, 8
School of Oriental & African
  Studies, 53
Schools, 34, 37, 42, 44, 45, 54,
  69-71, 148, 156, 168
Self-help programs, 153-155, 166
Shifta, 152

Slavery, 97, 108, 113, 161
Socialism, 134, 153, 165, 166, 169
Somali tribe, 15, 149, 152, 184
Somalia, 149, 152
Somerhough, Prosecutor, 94, 96-99
South Africa, 24, 52, 60, 146, 161, 178, 180
Soviet Union, 135, 149, 153, 159, 167, 185
Sporting events, 182
Squatters, 32, 37, 100, 137, 144, 154, 156-158, 166
Stalin, Joseph, 50
Storrington, 57
Strikes, 71, 72, 115, 116
Sudan, 148
Sultan of Zanzibar, 23
Swahili, 29, 38, 40, 63, 64, 82, 97, 134, 136, 140, 146, 156, 159

Taita tribe, 144
Tanzania, 18, 144, 151, 154, 180
Terrorism, see Atrocities
Thacker, Ransley N., 94-96, 98, 104, 105, 108
Thuku, Harry, 41-44, 58, 59, 83
Tourism, 181, 182
Trial, 93-99, 101, 104, 105, 118
Tribalism, 38, 65, 132, 134-137, 148, 149, 163, 164, 166, 183, 184
Turkana tribe, 122, 143

Udall, Stewart, 145
Uganda, 23, 101, 154, 180
Uhuru Day, see Independence Day
Uhuru Stadium, 142, 145
Unemployment, 32, 34, 37, 63, 73, 137, 154, 168-171
United Nations, 10, 134, 135, 137, 156, 161
United States, 7-9, 53, 59, 95, 119, 135, 142, 143, 146, 157, 159-161, 164, 167, 176, 180, 181, 185
Univ. of East Africa (Royal Coll.), 166
Univ. of London, 55
Univ. of Moscow, 53

Waiyaki, Chief, 23, 24
Wa Kiano, Gikonyo, 107
Ward, Alex., 184
Waruhiu, Chief, 87, 88
Watu wa Mungu (People of God), 45, 54
Weeping Kamau, the, 157
Weimar Republic, 50
Western Powers, 133, 147, 159-161, 164, 166, 167, 171, 175
White emigration, 142, 157, 182
White Highlands, 11, 12, 24-26, 33, 36, 39-41, 73, 77, 86, 91, 92, 99, 101, 103, 105, 111, 120, 123, 144, 145, 156, 170, 182
White population, 22, 24-27, 29, 33, 34, 37, 39-41, 43, 59, 62, 64, 65, 73, 74, 79-81, 85, 86, 88, 92-95, 97, 98, 101, 103, 112, 113, 115-117, 120, 121, 123, 127, 131, 132, 136, 137, 139-141, 145, 148, 157, 170, 176-178, 181, 182, 184
Williams, G. Mennen, 143
Witch doctors, 18-21, 28, 47, 158
Woodbrooke, 51
Workers' Educ. Assoc., 57
World War I, 38
World War II, 57, 64

Young Kikuyu Assoc. (YKA), 41, 43, 44
Young Wingers, 168, 170
Youth Brigade, 154
Youth programs, 135, 142, 143, 154, 160, 185

192